He knew that the Hebrews were looking for a key to life that would enable them to show forth healthy bodies, kingly raiment, richer living and a secure existence. Their minds were focused on what they would eat, where they would live and how they would be clothed. Seeing their error, he urged them to give up this frantic search for the fruits of the Spirit and seek Spirit Itself. "Seek ye first the Kingdom of God, and His righteousness; and all these things shall be added unto you" (Luke 12:31). Seek first and foremost the consciousness of God – the realization of God's omnipresence – and all that God *is* will be manifestly present in your life. Ask for the consciousness of God. Seek it exclusively. If necessary knock for it repeatedly. Knock and knock and knock again. The door of direct revelation will surely be opened to you. *"For every one that asketh receiveth* (the Kingdom)*; and he that seeketh findeth* (the Kingdom)*; and to him that knocketh it* (the door of revelation) *shall be opened"* (Luke 11:10). This is an eternal promise.

Our words and actions betray what manner of belief governs us. Are you still trying to work out some problem? Are your efforts directly related to food, shelter and clothing? Are you more concerned about getting ahead in life than discovering what life really is? Are you afraid to seek first the Kingdom for fear that your basic needs will not be taken care of? Are you afraid that perhaps everything you have accumulated thus far will somehow be whisked away from you? Do you associate the single desire for revelation with poverty, limitation and restriction? Now is the time to jump *in toto* into the waters of spiritual enlightenment. Heretofore you may have waved your feet back and forth, timidly testing the waters. This is not the time to entertain doubt and fear. It is the time to forget all and push onward toward the goal of God realization and revelation. Forget what the fruits will bring. It is not uncommon these days for one striving to make a mark in his career to forsake all those things formerly important to him in order to accomplish his goal. He will knowingly or unknowingly forsake friends, family and recreation for the sole purpose of achievement. You must be that one-pointed, forgetting all things for the sole (soul) purpose of direct revelation.

Regardless of the questions you ask, the end result is always the same – the total and complete knowledge of God. This, of course, is total and complete Self-knowledge. One may begin living the life of revelation simply by asking God to reveal Himself. Many have done this, but they err in expecting revelation to fit within the narrow confines of previous conceptions. These very same people think they do much good simply because of their spiritual devotion, but their failure to receive anything of God is attributable to their service and devotion to an *idea* of God and not to God at all. They serve nothing and they get nothing. The Old Testament prophet cited, "They return, but not to the most High...."

In the story of the Prodigal Son (Luke 15:11-32), a great lesson is given of the unfruitful life realized by serving a false or unknown God. You are undoubtedly familiar with the account of the son who gathered up his inheritance and left home only to return when his dreams and expectations were shattered by the reality that life could not be lived securely, prosperously, joyously and freely away from his father's house. The mystical implications here are obvious, but focus the attention now upon the elder son who remained at home. When the father informed him that his lost brother had returned, it is written that he refused to take part in the planned celebration: *"Lo, these many years do I serve thee, neither transgressed I at any time thy commandment: and yet thou never gavest me a kid, that I might make merry with my friends: but as soon as this thy son was come, which hath devoured thy living with harlots, thou hast killed for him the fatted calf."* Note carefully the father's response to that faithful son: *"Son, thou art ever with me, and all that I have is thine."*

The fatted calf, the continual feast and eternal joy were ever the faithful son's. He failed to realize that all that the father had was *always* his and *always* available to him. You see, this son was not aware somehow of the special relationship he had with his father and his father's possessions. His thought was that perhaps *someday* he would be rewarded for all of his diligence, failing to realize that the day was always at hand and that he could have availed himself of the blessings of his choice at *any* time.

Long have we seemed to suffer from a distorted understanding of God and His Kingdom, thinking that perhaps the Kingdom would come *someday* for us, and that only *then* would we experience happiness, contentment, love, prosperity, wholeness and peace. To each of us seemingly under this spell of delay, the still small voice grows increasingly strong with shouts of glad hosannas, with messages of the Kingdom *now at hand*, with the good news that all that is God *is ours now*, that the fruits of the Spirit are ripe *at this very moment* to be taken and enjoyed.

My friend, how will these messages be made known to us? How will we recognize our freedom from delay, and know of a certainty that the highest fulfillment of our inner longings is *now at hand* to be experienced? We will know, each and every one of us, when we cease from our own sense of personal wisdom and gather all of our understanding and knowledge from inner revelation, inspiration and direct experience of Reality. This is the *only* way, and beside it there is no other. Many have hoped there would be another way that would allow them (in their distorted sense of identity as humans) to be participants and even helpers in enlightenment. They fancy that the assuming of strange physical postures, the mental recitation of "spiritual" words, the adherence to special diets and a host of other exercises of the human mind and body will gain them entrance into the heavenly realm. None of these things has revealed the Kingdom of heaven. None of these things ever will, because "no *man* can see the face of God and live" (as he lived formerly). "No man can see the face of God" (as a separate entity from himself). Only when empty from these false notions of God and of himself as an identity *separate* and *apart* from God will he experience God. Only God can experience God. GOD IS ALL THERE IS. There comes a certain moment in silent meditation that is hard to pinpoint. But at this time one is no longer aware of himself as he *formerly* has been aware of himself. At this oft-times imperceptible moment one has burst from self-imposed confinements and experiences the Divine as Reality – as the *only* Reality. He has seen the face of God and no longer lives the same as he lived before. All things seem somehow different. *Of course they are,* for in this revelation he has perceived that GOD IS ALL. No longer can he seem to suffer under the delusion that powers of disease, negativity, destruction, restriction and limitation are powers *at all*. He knows that GOD IS ALL and this knowing is indeed life-changing. Life is not changed from one state into another, but one begins to experience life as it is. What a glorious experience, regardless of how fleeting it may seem.

Much has been said about revelation and its importance. For many, this seems to be such unfamiliar territory that they have no idea what to look for in the experience. It will suffice to say that the experience of revelation can be as varied as the many manifestations of God's omnipresence. It is not always a voice, nor is it always brilliant flashes of light, and yet sometimes these do indeed occur. There are so many subtle ways in which God reveals Himself. Although the manifestations of revelation vary, one always knows with absolute certainty when the experience is a God experience. Where many founder is in hoping to duplicate the spiritual experience of another – a particular author, lecturer or friend. *Have your own.* Whatever way God reveals Himself is the way that is most suitable for you *at that point* in your experience. Honor your revelation. Relish it without hoping to exchange it for something more "valid." This is sometimes the case when God announces His presence as a deep, calm peace – a peace that surely passes beyond anything of human experience or understanding. Perhaps you have had this experience but did not count it as a "real" experience because there were no whirling lights or vivid colors. One experience is no more valid than another when one opens himself fully to the experience.

Again, it may seem as though God is revealing Himself to someone separate from His very own omnipresent being. This is not the case at all. Someone has explained it as *God revealing Himself to Himself.* If there be any revelation, this must be true. Certainly, it would be helpful to understand exactly what transpires in this experience of revelation. At the very point of revelation, the Mind of God, the only Mind, makes Itself known. The sense of personal mind with its limitations is dissolved and not even known or experienced. Eventually the time comes when this is a continual experience, but until that time arrives the experiences occur with seeming gaps between which begin to close with the increasing frequency of revelation and illumination. A word to the wise: when these moments of revelation come upon you, relax into them, open up to them, and let yourself fully experience your Self. Revelation is truly a marvelous experience each time, even though the experiences may vary.

Dear reader, you do understand now what takes place when you ask a question seeking light and revelation upon a specific subject. You do understand that the question is a catalyst for revelation, a catalyst for the experience of the only Mind as *your* Mind bringing with the experience the revelation that you seek. It is a truth that, even in this so-called process of questioning, the answers can be presented in very different ways. The answers may come as an audible voice or perhaps as a sudden stream of thoughts that run on without any personal guidance whatsoever. And there may be some experience that the author has not had that may be your very own experience. Never, *ever* limit yourself to previously known experiences. Just let the answers flow forth.

Often when an individual is seeking some specific revelation, that individual will call an "authority" asking for verification that he (or she) has indeed experienced Divine revelation. Invariably the caller will ask, "Was that God, or was that my own mind?" If you ever find yourself in such a quandary, do know for a certainty that you *have* no mind of your *own*; know too that the doubt is a signal that you need to keep up the questioning until the revelation comes and leaves you with no doubt whatsoever. It is often the case that one fails to persist in seeking direct revelation. Persistence and faith are so important and necessary, particularly if you have never before consciously experienced direct revelation.

While nothing else is assured you, revelation is. Trust in the fact that those who seek Truth for Truth's sake will most certainly be rewarded with Truth. With this in mind, be careful that you don't make the useless attempt to reason your way into revelation. It will not work. You will be left feeling empty and desolate. In many cases, because you have read so many books on Truth, there is an inclination in your meditations to rehash material from a favorite author, speaker or mentor, thinking this to be revelation. Once revelation is experienced, it is easy to detect when there is an attempt to reason your way into revelation. Prior to this initial experience, you will be warned by the feeling of incompletion that accompanies everything that the human mind concocts.

At the moment of revelation, do not make the mistake many make just then of being so overcome with the thrill of the experience that you do not allow yourself time to *live* with the experience and actually *be* the experience. So often there is the tendency to jump up immediately with joy and excitement. *Stay there until the entire experience has completed itself.* Of course, there is a point where the experience will be eternal. Expect that to be so with you, but if that is not your present experience, be sure to fully live out the current experience.

Do not believe for one moment that the present revelation is the final revelation. Very often, questions lead to more questions. In an ecstatic moment, God reveals Himself as all there is. GOD IS ALL. You have heard it before. You have read it before, and probably you have recited it for several years. *Now you know it.* What a wonderful, freeing feeling it is to actually *know* that God is All. But what does this wonderful annunciation *mean*? Your next question may simply be "What does `God is All' mean?" Soon another revelation comes forth more glorious than the previous one, and yet it too may lead to other questions. Keep up with this until your questions are answered. Will there ever be an end to these questioning periods? You will discover the answer to this for yourself. Just simply be committed to seeing and being Truth Itself.

In seeking wisdom directly, never for one moment believe there is unwillingness on God's part to reveal Himself. Never believe for an instant that God has anything to do with the seeming failure to experience direct revelation. Frequently, it is the case that one's disbelief in the *possibility* of this experience *delays* the experience. At other times, it is a sense of unworthiness that seems to thwart the experience. For many, it is the idea of God coming down from somewhere into something other than Himself that seems to be the barrier. Remember, you are not trying to contact God. You are not trying to get wisdom from someone *outside* of your very own being. You are simply experiencing your Self as you ARE.

Suppose that you find yourself asking a particular question and there seems to be a sense of restlessness with that question. It may seem that you just can't fully "get into" that question. All right. This question is not your question. It is not the revelation that is announcing itself to you at this moment. Keep on with this question, however. It is your "leader" question. It will lead you to that question whose answer is now coming forth. There are other times when you simply are not able to settle into any question. This too is fine. These are times when you are to just remain still, listening and watching as the revelations pour forth on their own accord. Always remember to allow yourself to BE the experience of the revelations that come forth. This is of utmost importance.

In asking questions of your God Consciousness, the repeated attempts that so often seem necessary to receiving answers to your questions serve only to move you beyond present belief systems that are not in accord with the enlightenment soon to come. It is not that there are two minds here, a resistant mind and an all-knowing Mind. Rather, the case is that a seeming belief in a personal mind has established its own belief system. This is no mind at all, and once one realizes this, the revelations come forth more quickly and with less effort. Whenever there seems to be an undue delay in revelation, let it count for naught but a seeming resistance to know what is about to be imparted.

There is one other instance when revelation seems delayed, and it warrants a paragraph – perhaps even a book – to itself. The most frustrating and exasperating delays take place when one attempts to apply Truth to some unfavorable appearance in an effort to heal or improve it in some way. All of this questioning business is about seeing things *as they are* and *always have been* in Eternity. If your involvement in this practice is for the purpose of helping and healing, it is perhaps better that you engage in some other "spiritual" practice that has "healing" and "improving" built into its system. In the system of Truth nothing needs healing or improving; therefore, the vain attempts to use Truth as a healing agent meet with disappointing results. How often do we ask a question about the body in a desperate attempt to heal it? Do we not ask questions about supply, not to fully understand it but with the hope that our wallets and bank accounts will fatten up? Truth must be sought for *Truth's sake only*, for the joy of *knowing* and knowing that you know. The usual response to such statements is, "That's fine, but I want something that will work in my life, something that will improve my lot in life." Truth revealed will not improve your life, it will not heal your life, and will not work in your life. Truth *will* reveal the flawless Kingdom that *is* your life – in need of no works, healings or demonstrations. However, what is revealed in secret is evidenced, and this is what is objectively called healing or improvement. But you, having received this glorious revelation, know that nothing has changed, nothing has been healed and nothing has been improved.

How often should you keep asking a particular question? The answer is simple. Keep *asking and asking and asking* until revelation springs forth. Never settle for anything less than revelation. Be like the persistent widow in the parable of Jesus. You are not just asking one question at a time. Perhaps during any given period, you are asking several questions. But with each question, you are giving your utmost attention to "listening" for the answer. Do not let this process become a struggle or an effort. When you find impatience and struggle entering into your meditations, proceed to the next question. You will automatically know when to end each session. Regardless of the seeming, something has happened with each of your questioning sessions. You will even begin to see "external" changes just from the process of questioning. At a later time in the day you will again have another session devoted to direct revelation. This seems to be a most passive exercise indeed. Never mind this. For all its seeming passivity, this is probably the most powerful activity in which you can involve yourself.

Does the foregoing imply that you are to never step inside a church again, never read a book again, never again attend a lecture? No. It *does* mean that your purpose for doing any of these things is no longer that of *learning* anything. By all means do all of these, but realize that there is nothing that you can hear that you do not *already* know. Realize also that you cannot live off the revelations of any minister, author or lecturer. You can only live by your own revelations. This is so very important to understand.

As a final note of encouragement, it must be said that there are times when revelation does not seem forthcoming. Regardless of your best attempts to "see" more, all appears to be in vain. Although it has only been a few days, it seems like a lifetime. All begins to seem dark and dismal. Perhaps there is even a slight inclination to believe that the entire practice has been futile. You may even think that you have fabricated your spiritual experiences and that they were the result of an overactive and hopeful imagination. All is well in your affairs, but somehow all seems confusing and somewhat depressing. Everything is working, yet nothing seems to be working. This is the time to rely on your past experiences for encouragement. Looking at them straight on, you know they were real. Realize now that revelation can and will happen again. Recapture the feeling of joy and excitement that accompanied those initial revelations. Contemplate those revelations. Ask questions that will lead to greater awareness of that which you already know to be Truth. It is helpful to know that these "dry spells" usually occur when one is seeking some specific outcome or sign as evidence of one's revelations.

I recall in my own experience a time when I was asking questions regarding money and wealth. This was at a point when I realized that I seemed to know nothing at all about money – spiritually speaking. I would ask my Self questions such as, "What is money?" "What is the spiritual significance of money?" "What is my relationship to money?" "What is wealth?" Revelations did begin to stream forth concerning many of the questions I asked. Notwithstanding, I saw nothing of significance that bore witness to the wonderful revelations I had received. My next question was, "What is the evidence that I am wealth?" I asked this question repeatedly until something came forth. Finally, what revealed itself were these words of Christ Jesus: *"A wicked and adulterous generation seeketh after a sign; and there shall no sign be given unto it, but the sign of the prophet Jonas"* (Matthew 12:39). I had read this statement in the Bible several times and never quite understood the latter part of it. This was a crucial moment, and it was essential that I come to terms with that which I seemed not to understand. Jonah of course was imprisoned in the darkness of the fish's belly. The darkness of disease, poverty, death and destruction are also prisons. Immediately it came forth that the only sign for sign-seekers would be more of the same and worse of their present plight; for they believed in Truth *and* some other condition. The revelation seemed not the *full* Truth for them. What followed was another revelation with Scripture intermingled: *"I am my own evidence and beside me there is no other."*

*Revelations are Truth.* Truth cannot be applied to that which is not Truth. For that which is not Truth is *nothing at all.* Truth is not opposed to a seeming condition. Truth reveals that the *seeming* is nothing at all. It disperses the agglutination of the nothingness called matter to reveal the finished Kingdom of Truth. It is so important to live with your revelations as *Truth,* and as the *only* Truth. Forget signs and evidence. As long as you look for signs to support your revelations, you are still operating under the erroneous assumption that there is something other than Truth. Under this assumption, no sign can be given. It was suggested earlier that you BE your revelations. Only Truth can experience Truth. When a revelation comes forth, do not stop there, but allow the revelation to *be* you, for it *is* you. Discouragement and frustration are the rewards of sign-seekers. Be content with Truth and Truth *alone*.

# CHAPTER TWO

# The Lord's Prayer

*"Our Father, which art in heaven, Hallowed be thy name. Thy kingdom come. Thy will be done in earth, as it is in heaven. Give us this day our daily bread. And forgive us our debts, as we forgive our debtors. And lead us not into temptation; but deliver us from evil: For thine is the kingdom, and the power, and the glory, for ever. Amen"* (Matthew 6:9-13).

Throughout the history of Christianity, these words have been repeated over and over by the Christian masses, often in the hope that their mere repetition would generate a special, spiritual power over some supposed negative circumstance. Is this prayer unique and "special"? Has the mere recitation of it come forth with any real power? If so, the millions who have recited it for the last two thousand years would have generated enough "spiritual power" to totally annihilate all appearances of evil. But that has not been the case. It is, however, the *understanding* of the words of this prayer which yield true satisfaction and evidence supporting its words.

It was during the "Sermon On The Mount" when the disciples asked Him, "Lord, teach us to pray," that Christ Jesus gave what is now known as the "Lord's Prayer." It is written in Matthew 6:9 that Jesus tells them to pray "after this manner" and then presents the familiar words. Does the prayer have magic in and of itself? No. Does the repetition of these words yield anything? No, for vain repetitions are the practice of heathens. To pray in the manner of the Lord's Prayer is to pray with full understanding of its component verses.

## Our Father

In the time of Jesus the Christ, the father was unquestionably the head of the household, sole provider, governor of the familial estate, sustainer and chief executive. When rightly viewed, God is the sole provider of this universe, head of His omnipresent Kingdom, the sole sustainer, the sole governing Law and the sole executor.

God, as we have stated many times over, is indeed All in All and All as All. Indisputably, God is head of the household of heaven; for God and *only God* is present in heaven – the heaven *all about us*. If we would truly understand this Truth of One Presence, we would understand our own and only identity. We can no longer judge by the appearances of separate identities, bodies and objects. To see ONE, we must judge by the ONE.

God is the sole provider. What else is there? The understanding of this is true liberation from dependency on external sources for supply and sustenance. Failing economies, temporary or permanent layoffs, factory shutdowns, stock market crashes and the like would mean nothing to us, once we perceived that God is the sole (only) provider in His omnipresent Kingdom. For whom is God providing? The answer to this question as revealed within your very own consciousness would be to you the equivalent of a never-failing bank account. With *what* is God providing anyone or anything? The answer to this question is the understanding of substance. Substance is provision. God is substance. God is supply.

God as the governor of his estate governs according to His law of ONENESS, "ONLYNESS", SINGLENESS. Take a good look at that word ONE. Where can there be confusion, division, violence, destruction, war, criminal behavior, disease and so on in ONE SINGLE SOLITARY EXISTENCE? You are absolutely right to conclude that the Law of God must be a Law of Love, a Law of Peace, a Law of Harmony; changeless and eternal.

Granted, none of these things *appears* to be so. Violence, destruction and disease seem to be the order of the day. Again my friend, you are asked to "judge not according to appearances" but to judge only according to the Law of the One. At a point of God-Realization, you indeed will be certain of one thing: GOD IS ALL THERE IS. Once you are certain of this, Life will be perceived as it really is. The *"terror by night"* shall not move thee; nor *"the arrow that flieth by day"*; nor *"the pestilence that walketh in darkness"*; nor *"the destruction that wasteth at noonday. A thousand shall* (appear) *to fall at thy side, and ten thousand at thy right hand; but it shall not come nigh thee.... Because thou hast made the Lord* (the Law of GOD IS ALL)*... thy habitation..."* (Psalm 91:5-9).

It is commonly the case that people come to God in their extremity seeking to fill some void in their lives. Often they are in need of greater income and desire a surefire blueprint for success. Even the "Thoughts Are Things" movement that abounds to this day has failed to present a principle ensuring success. Christ Jesus provided the key long ago. Perhaps His formula was ignored because He was not viewed as a success. However, according to the records He had a most auspicious beginning. From the day of His birth His life was threatened by the ruling powers who feared the influence He would someday wield on society. Here is one who taught rabbis in the temple even as a child, already quite successful in His command of Hebrew lore. Here is a man who never had a family of His own to feed, but at a moment's notice could prepare a meal for thousands – minus cooking utensils, minus help and unhindered by time. Would you call that successful? Here is a man who never had medical training; and yet *instantly* He could heal the incurable. When death made its claims decimating families, He could come with the calm assurance that what appeared as death was just sleep – and call the dead back to life again. Is this successful enough for you? Perhaps it would take this final triumph to convince you that no other living being is recorded as having been so utterly successful in abiding by his own contrived "success secrets." It was the participation in His own death and destruction and then the presentation of His resurrected physical body to His friends – to prove that death and destruction were not in the omnipresent Kingdom – that was Jesus the Christ's supreme demonstration of successful achievement. What could be more successful than the demonstration that there is no power on earth – not even death itself – that can destroy the I AM that I AM?

In John 5:30 and 14:10 is found the key to Jesus's success: *"I can of mine own self do nothing." "...The Father that dwelleth in me, he doeth the works."* Can you for one second imagine God failing at anything? You cannot honestly answer this with a "yes." It seems so simple, doesn't it – *just let God do it.* It is more, so much more than this. It is this idea of "just let God do it" that has sustained mounting frustration with unsuccessful efforts. GOD IS NOT GOING TO DO IT THROUGH YOU OR FOR YOU. GOD IS NOT HAVING ANY INVOLVEMENT WITH YOU WHAT-SOEVER. By this I mean that God does not see a channel *outside of His very own omnipresence* to work with or for. My friend, we must walk all the way with this Truth of GOD IS ALL. For God to be truly all, there can be nothing for God to work *with*, *through*, *for*, or – as some have believed – *against*.

To understand these statements made by Christ Jesus, we must cease forever to think of an identity *other* than God. Furthermore, we must include our very own being in this ONE IDENTITY. Many have understood the opening words of the Lord's Prayer to imply duality. They have thought these words spoken by Christ Jesus – "Our Father" – to be similar to the relationship a son would have with his father. There is no duality, there are no dual identities in this statement. Jesus clarified His relationship with the Father with these words: "...He that hath seen me hath seen the Father...." "I and my Father are one." In some branches of metaphysical teaching, there is projected a false doctrine of which Jesus is the supposed author that proclaims, "I am one with God." Do you see the implication of two identities here? However, "I and my Father are one," which is the statement of Christ Jesus, implies one identity viewed from different angles. One time the identity is viewed as the Father, another time this very same identity is viewed as the Son, yet it is ever the same identity.

With a full understanding of the foregoing Truth, it is easy to say all that God is, *you* are, and all that God is *not*, you are not. But this statement cannot be mere lip service. It must come with a real understanding of what God *is* and what God *is not*. A book cannot teach this to you. A minister cannot give you this awareness. It must come as revelation from within your very own being. You probably know people who have read every book on the shelf about the nature of God, yet their lives have not evidenced anything similar to what they so doggedly read in book after book after book. Knowledge cannot be imparted from external sources. It can only be revealed from its very own dwelling place – your consciousness.

The entire biological theory of genetics is here put to rest with the words "Our Father." Such inherited traits as intelligence, beauty (or the apparent lack thereof), diseases, baldness, temperament and so on are seen for the fiction they are. "Call no man on earth your Father," Jesus advised those who had need of escape from hereditary entrapments. Just the realization that you have no earthly father to inherit anything from is freedom itself. Here you are left face to face with being the perfection that God, your Father, your Self, *is* right now.

This entire scene of racial upheaval, based upon appearances of discrimination, must be seen for what it is. I will not venture to name it anything; rather, I will leave it to you to discover whether there can be any truth in it whatsoever. Howbeit, certain points must be considered here. This "Our Father" applies to every living, moving, breathing creature of this universe. It applies one hundred percent to them *all*. God is one hundred percent Himself the Father – as we have now come to understand this term – of every man, woman and child in this universe, regardless of the varying appearances of race and color. They all inherit one hundred percent of all that the "Father" is. It is the individual realization of our right and true relationship with God that will be our real freedom. And the freedom realized will be such that no man can put asunder. Can God be imprisoned? Can God be discriminated against? Can God be ill-favored? Can God be victimized? He who seeth you seeth the Father.

In John 4:24 it is written, *"God is spirit, and those who worship him must worship him in spirit and truth."* You are spirit. You *must* be; for God is all there is of you. This is no revolutionary statement. You have seen it, read it and said it many times; but have you ever really pondered the full implications of that statement? Have you ever really questioned your Self about what it means to *be* Spirit? Certainly you know that it means you are not matter or material. The laws of matter are foreign to you by virtue of your own Divinity. The laws of restriction, limitation, degeneration, depletion and decay are *not* a part of Spirit. They are *not* a part of you. You really *are* the free life of Spirit. There are absolutely no laws to encumber you. In the realm of Spirit, which is the only realm (all else is fiction), there are no laws. Here there is absolutely no need for laws. Laws govern something. Here there is nothing but Spirit – nothing else to govern. Here Spirit is self-governing. The government truly is upon the shoulders of one who identifies himself as the very presence of the Father that hath sent him.

You probably have noted with interest that Jesus did not teach that God is the *Mother* of all the universe, but the Father. Have you questioned your Self as to *why*? In the traditional family structure and in the tradition of biological theory, a male (father) and female (mother) together produce an offspring. Here you have two separate entities joining together to produce a third entity. In the Kingdom of God that is now at hand there is only One. Jesus called this One "Father." There is no room in omnipresence for two-ness; therefore, no mother was mentioned. He could have referred to the Spirit that is God as "Mother" just as easily; however, there would then be no mention of Father. There is no duality in the Kingdom.

Now we are approaching treacherous grounds. Did God mate with someone or something to produce your being? Of course not. There is nothing or no one in the Kingdom but God. Was God created? Of course not. You and the Father are one and the same. I and the Father are one and the same. Were you and I created? If we were created, it must have been by something other than our own identity. If we were created by something other than our own identity, then the I that I AM is not all that there is. Do not let these statements disturb you; but rather, approach them with an open mind. Ask the very presence of wisdom that dwells in and as your own consciousness these questions. Ask and ask and ask again until the revelation comes forth. It is imperative that we live not by speculation but solely through revelation.

## Who Art in Heaven

Here again there is much that requires personal discovery for one to perceive the practicality inherent in these four words. *Heaven* means *Cause*. Here Christ Jesus is teaching the disciples that God is Cause Itself. Furthermore, God is the ONLY CAUSE. It is imperative that this be understood and that all its implications be revealed. Under the three circuits of living, there are various reasons given for the effects that seem to appear in this universe. From the physical perspective, in earlier times an understanding of the sciences was thought to give one a greater clue to living more fully and effectively in this world. However, science remained riddled with so many unanswered questions that something else was believed needed. This led to the science of metaphysics. Under this mental circuit of living, everything was reduced to the nature and quality of thoughts held in mind. Poverty was linked to limited thinking. Illness was attributed to wrong thinking. For example, cancer was said to be caused by negative emotions long-sustained by the individual – strong emotions usually identified as hate, anger and resentment. Eczema was said to result from a feeling of being unloved or unwanted by one or both parents. Success was believed assured by entertaining successful thoughts, and health guaranteed by holding thoughts of wholeness. Everything was reduced to thoughts and thinking.

Mental metaphysics left much to be desired. First of all, the required discipline to always hold positive thoughts was and is too demanding. Secondly, the idea that one would be held accountable for every negative thought has proved unnerving to most. Lastly, in many instances it became next to impossible to trace the offending thought that produced the unwanted condition. Again, something more was thought necessary. This "something more" was a way of living that did not involve the participation of man *with* God but the existence of man *as* God.

We must realize that we cannot continue to proclaim the omnipotence of God and also continue to proclaim that human thoughts and words have power as well. "A house divided... cannot stand." God alone is power. There is no power in a positive thought or negative thought. This alone leaves God to be power. This makes null and void any sense of personal power. If my thoughts have no power and my words have no power, what am I to do? Nothing. "I can of mine own self do nothing."

God alone is Cause and there is no effect. Do understand that in order for there to be cause and effect there would have to be *two*, or at very best an interim of time in the timeless. Yes, God is Cause, but this is correctly interpreted to mean that God is the *cause of His own existence.* Nothing has caused God to exist. Nothing will cause God to cease to exist throughout His omnipresent Kingdom.

## Hallowed Be Thy Name

Simply put, the nature of God is wholeness and completeness. If God were not whole and complete, *from what would God acquire His wholeness and completeness*? These four words "Hallowed be thy name" require personal discovery concerning their full meaning and practicality in your everyday living experience. The true understanding of these words would entirely alter your living pattern. It would provide a sense of freedom and independence never before imagined or experienced.

At some point one must begin to question what the completeness of God has specifically to do with *who I am*, *what I presently know*, *what I have* and *what I do not have*. You will probably ask something like this: "In the image and likeness of God (as correctly understood), am I already complete, lacking nothing?" Other questions will undoubtedly arise. However, it is essential that you wait for the revelation of answers to these questions. A growing realization of your own completeness will totally alter your relationships, whether romantic or platonic. Most relationships seem to be symbiotic. But you, aware of your own fullness, your own wholeness, can entertain relationships expressing real and true Love. This is the Love that does not seek after its own from anyone. This is the Love that does not puff up or behave itself unseemly because of a perceived need or lack. This is the Love that rejoices in the Truth of complete and whole existence everywhere present.

## Thy Kingdom Come

All living souls in this universe, if they admit their souls' sincere desire, would like to behold and experience the Kingdom of God *here* and *now* while they yet move, live and breathe upon this earth. All of this human movement and busyness is nothing but the vain attempt to approximate what they suspect life in the Kingdom would be like. Certainly they suspect it would be free from monetary concerns, so they work hard to achieve a sense of financial freedom. It is suspected also that in this vast, vast Kingdom would be a glorious sense of love; and so they desperately seek out relationship after relationship, hoping to approximate what they have determined love to be. These very same beings entertain the correct notion that living in the Kingdom would be a life of untold joy and ecstasy; and so through party-throwing and party-going in the hope of finding that joy, through the abuse of all sorts of substances for the thrill of that expected ecstasy, and through excessive sexual activity, they have constructed a counterfeit Kingdom. Their reasoning extends yet further. Would not the Kingdom be free from disease, disaster and violence? Of course. So the busyness of humans erects hospitals, educational institutions and laboratories in the hope of conquering disease, and maintains criminal institutions with assigned prison cells to stave off destruction by violence.

These efforts have proved fruitless. Speaking on the side of the appearances of things, the world seems to be moving toward its own destruction. Why has not all this busyness produced the hoped-for results? Why is it that after one disease is conquered another springs up, seemingly more life threatening than the last? Why do crime and substance abuse seem to escalate despite great and noble attempts to eradicate both of these? The reason for all of these appearances – and that is just exactly what they are – is that the activity is based upon the false assumption that the Kingdom is not *already here* and must be either produced or approximated.

It was in the town of Capernaum that Jesus began preaching, and his first words were: *"Repent: for the kingdom of heaven is at hand."* What a lovely and comforting assurance to know – really know – that the Kingdom of heaven is at hand; to know that *while*

*I yet walk upon this earth, I walk in the finished kingdom of heaven.* The Pharisees, the Sadducees, the disciples and the entire population – except an enlightened few – were all waiting for a coming Kingdom that would allow them rest from their labors. It seemed to them afar off or perhaps never to come at all. Then a stranger arrived in their midst proclaiming that the long-awaited Kingdom "is now at hand." Unending joy was not something afar off *but at hand.* Abiding love needed no longer to be anticipated but *was presently at hand.* Wholeness, prosperity, success and comfort were qualities of life *now to be enjoyed.* How does this sound to you – you who are the living embodiment of all these? That is exactly how it sounded to those who initially heard the message of The Christ.

The word "repent" means to change the mind. Here metaphysicians have grossly erred in thinking that to "change the mind" means to repeat over and over a conglomeration of positive statements in the hope of spiritualizing the consciousness. If a negative thought is taking hold, they immediately replace it with a positive thought in order to cancel the effects of the negative thought. All of this symbolizes repentance to the metaphysician. Let's examine the fallacy of all this mental busyness. The *only* spiritual consciousness is the consciousness of God. This has been called by many the Divine Mind. It is the Mind that announces that *"...my thoughts are not your* (human mind) *thoughts...."* This is the changeless Mind of God; furthermore, it is the very changeless Presence of God. GOD IS ALL, EVEN AS MIND. If we are going to accept the changeless nature of God, we are going to have to accept that Divine Mind has never become a human mind and also that a human mind can never *ever* become Divine. For all of this *becoming,* you see, connotes a change of some sort. All of the positive thoughts entertained by a mind perceived to be human is nothing but a human mind with positive thoughts. It is not the Divine Mind that IS the glorious presence of God. The first indication of the truth of these statements is the failure of positive thinking to produce the desired results, coupled with the great effort required to maintain these thoughts consistently. Do you think that God is struggling to maintain positive thoughts? Do you believe that God thinks at all? Do you think that it is a great effort for God to behold His omnipresence? Do you think that anything supposedly less than God can behold God, or can enter into His courts? This spiritual consciousness that the metaphysicians are seeking is the very Consciousness that is God. Their futile efforts are unknowingly for the sole purpose of discovering that this Mind is really *their very own* Mind. This is Truth. There is only ONE MIND and ONE CONSCIOUSNESS.

It has often been stated that "Life is Consciousness." This is true. However, this statement has been distorted to suggest that the life of each individual is solely dependent upon *his* consciousness and its comprising thoughts. By this law, the person who has more consistently held positive thoughts in mind has demonstrated a life more closely approximating the Kingdom of heaven. The person who has entertained hosts of negative thoughts has, by this law, created for himself the proverbial hell. What is wrong here? How many creative powers are there? Is God the single cause of all existence and the sole power of this universe, or does each individual wield his or her own personal power, rendering the omnipotence of God to no avail? If each individual has personal power, what happens to the omnipresence of God, the allness of God and the onlyness of God? These questions need to be answered, and they need to be answered within your own Consciousness. Revelation regarding these questions will free you from the belief of personal identity, karma and its supposed effects, and impart to you a new and true perspective of eternal life.

Life is Consciousness. However, Life is the Consciousness of God, the fount of Truth that cannot send forth both sweet and bitter water. Only the Consciousness of God is manifested. Only the Presence of God is manifested. Only God Is. God is entirely conscious of His Kingdom as an ever-present Kingdom, a *now* Kingdom, a Kingdom without end or interruption. This is your consciousness. This is the consciousness of the entire universe.

To repent in the true sense of the word does not mean to *change* the mind (for a changed human mind is still a human mind), but rather, to "exchange" the mind. Forfeit this counterfeit mind called a human mind with its worries, concerns and frustrations. Give up the belief that you have such a mind. Let the mind of God, Divine Mind, be realized to be your Mind, and your only Mind right now, this very moment. If you are totally willing for this revelation to come forth, it will; and it will be a completely natural, effortless and joyous coming forth. It will be a triumphant coming forth. The hosts of negative thoughts you have heretofore wrestled with under the law of mental metaphysics will no longer be your mental opponents. They will be seen for the nothingness that they are. More and more you will find yourself thinking whole, peaceful, prosperous, loving and joyous thoughts automatically. What's more, you will go even further than that by just *being* peace, prosperity, love and joy. Beloved, the KINGDOM IS AT HAND.

In the Gospel according to St. Matthew, we find Jesus giving the disciples the key to attaining *in this lifetime* the fulfillment of their hearts' desires: *"But seek ye first the kingdom of God, and his righteousness; and all these things shall be added unto you"* (Matthew 66:33). Do understand this to mean "seek first the consciousness of God." This is very much like Paul's message to the Philippians urging them to "have the mind of Christ, who thought it not robbery to be equal with God." With this urging of Jesus comes the promise that all who ask for this consciousness, all who seek this consciousness, and all who knock for it will indeed be rewarded with this consciousness. The renewing of the mind is not the attempt to make an old mind new through silly mental exercises and thought control; rather it is to realize the individual mind to be a focal point of the Divine Mind. This is the Mind that knows no evil, thinks no evil, sees no evil and believes no evil.

There is an old law of metaphysics that is totally inescapable, but it needs to be considered more closely so that the beauty of its message may be enjoyed. The law basically states that whatever is in the mind is in the experience – your experience. Does the Mind that is God have within Its omnipresence one impure thought or idea? You, having the Mind of Christ, equal with God, could no more know evil than could God. The beauty of this message is in the fact that having the Mind of God is having the experience of God, free of discord, strife, negativity, stress and discomfort. This is life and life more abundantly. Having abandoned the belief in a personal and separate mind, you behold the Divine Mind and gladly proclaim as did Christ Jesus, *"Repent: for the kingdom of heaven is at hand."*

There are certain times, resulting from a disciplined prayer life, when one is completely aware of the Kingdom now at hand. During these ecstatic moments one is supremely joyous. There's a lilt in the step, a glow on the face and a sense of true freedom never *ever* before experienced. At these times, there are literally no crooked places to be made straight. There are no "external" distractions of discord to claim the attention. Everything is dissolved and only God Is.

How long this ecstasy will last cannot be gauged. Ultimately, it is to be seen, experienced and revealed as our *only* state of existence. Subsequently, however, times follow when all seems dark, all seems lost and all of life seems futile and pointless. This period, no matter how brief, can seem to so rivet the attention that most (but never all) of that which was experienced before is forgotten. What does one do?

It is *here* and *now* that one must be mindful of the country out of which he came. You do know that the Kingdom is at hand. Though all seems lost *presently*, you *do* know what you *know*. Certainly it is not for you to attempt to recapture that last experience of the Kingdom. Yet it is imperative that you remain totally open to experience the Kingdom in newer and greater ways.

## Thy Will Be Done

Much has been said and written about the importance of letting God's will be done and of moving aside so that God may better work through us. I hope, beloved one, that you have examined these and similar statements and detected the falsity in them.

Have you ever noticed that this "moving aside" and "letting God's will be done" is never quite achieved, or at best must be done over and over again? Doesn't it seem that if "moving over," stepping aside or whatever it takes to have God's will be done proved effective, one would remain out of the way? Usually, despite perceiving the necessity of getting out of the way, the attempting one meets with failure or protracted struggle.

Most people who believe in God at all believe in a God of great power. Those further along are willing to state that God is the only power. Still further along "the way," there are those who believe God is the only Presence and only Power; and yet they continuously speak of getting out of God's way, so that God can work through them. No matter which of the foregoing you ascribe to, it would seem that all of a sudden God is this weakling who needs us to decide to move somewhere so He can act. Do you see the insanity of this type of thinking? If God is the Only Power, what power do humans have to be in the way of God? If God is the Only Presence and Power, who is there to be in the way needing to get out of the way? Herein is a good opportunity to examine what it is that you do indeed believe. It is an even greater opportunity through revelation to discover *what is true*.

Jesus had already proclaimed that *"the kingdom of God is at hand"*; but finding it necessary to elaborate upon this message, He further proclaimed that God's will is the will that is *being* done right now. What probably was not understood was that this will of God is not a will being done alongside some *other* will, but is surely the *only* will being done. It would be wise to replace the word "will" with "way" (Thy way is done). In Isaiah 55:8 the prophet declares, *"For my thoughts are not your thoughts, neither are your ways my ways, saith the Lord."* The way of humans is not the Way of God. The way of competition, backbiting and back-stabbing is not the Way of God. The way of living by the sweat of the brow is not the Way of God. The way of fear, the way of death and the way of poverty are not the ways of the Way. However, it is necessary to perceive that the Way of God is the only activity that is active. Does this mean that both evil and good emanate from God? How else, one might ask, can the appearances of evil be explained? They cannot be explained. Knowing something of the nature of God, one would not entertain these questions. Knowing something of the nature of God, one would leave appearances alone entirely, or at least recognize them for what they are. Jesus knew that until His congregation had totally realized the omnipresence of God, they would see things contrary to the Truth of existence. Thus He warned them, *"Judge not according to the appearance, but judge righteous judgment."*

It is the *appearance* of things that convinces one that God is not all there is. It is the *appearance* of things that convinces one that there is power in the cyclone, power in the virus and power in the nuclear bomb. What convinces you of poverty and insufficiency? Is it not *appearances*? GOD IS ALL. THE ENTIRE UNIVERSE IS NOUGHT BUT THE PRESENCE OF GOD. GOD IS THE ONLY ENTITY INHABITING THIS GREAT UNIVERSE AND THERE IS NO PRESENCE, WILL OR POWER BESIDE.

It is the seeming failure to perceive the Kingdom of God *now at hand* that causes people to speak of God's Will as some future event that promises good. It is the great misunderstanding of this line of the Lord's prayer, *"Thy will be done,"* that has caused many to put off the experience of their good *now at hand* and project it into some future time. One in the midst of bodily disease will say, "If it be God's will, I shall get better." You see, this one has put the experience of the wholeness of God *now at hand* into some future time, if at all. The Way of God is now at hand *presently being done* and it is the only Way being done. All else is nothing.

It has been suggested in many religious practices that the best way to experience the grace of God is to surrender unreservedly to the will of God. This is wonderful advice, but it does not go far enough and can even be quite misleading. The implication here is that one can choose to oppose the will of God, that one is something "of himself" and able to choose other than the will (way) of God; that there is another will operative in this universe and that God cannot possibly be all there is. If we are going to acknowledge the *allness of God*, we cannot talk of ourselves or others as something other than the very presence of God now acting as the will of God. The understanding of this is so very important. I recall my early years as a practitioner. Practitioners were always told – and I understand this still holds true in many metaphysical circles – never to begin treatment unless it was directly requested, or consent was obtained from the person to be treated. The reasoning behind this was that to do otherwise would be an infringement upon the right of that person to choose to remain in the condition he appeared to be in. For example, if John Doe had cancer, I could not begin to treat unless he made the request for treatment directly – or somehow consented to it – because John might choose to remain in this state of seeming illness (for whatever reason). To proceed without John's consent would violate his God-given freedom of choice. Let's examine the fallacy of such reasoning. John Doe is the very presence of God, a focal point of God's omnipresence. This will never change, regardless of appearances to the contrary. John was not given free will. If so, God would not be all. To *give* implies twoness. John is the free will (way) of God in action. However, this will knows nothing of tumors, cancerous tissues, degenerative diseases and the like. It knows free, unrestricted, uninhibited and unlimited activity. *This* is free will. It is the way and activity of God being unencumbered by the supposed laws and powers of matter. No one has *being* of one's own to have a will of one's own.

There are vast implications here. Do you know that there is not a being on this earth – in this universe – who has the free choice and free will to cause harm to "another," to block the free activity of God in and as "another?" Promotions cannot be blocked, success cannot be stymied and progress cannot be limited by another. There is no power in limitation. There *is* no *other*. A true realization of the Onlyness and Allness of God is truly a liberating experience to be enjoyed throughout your eternal life.

We do ourselves a great disservice when we seem to believe in the power of others to withhold our good in any way. We then no longer speak on the side of omnipotence and omnipresence. We no longer behold the single Presence of God. We no longer find ourselves free to be our Self. We begin thinking in terms of two-ness, evil, destruction, foreign powers and an impotent God. Do you see that to speak of another's power to block our progress is to see him *outside* of the omnipresence of God? The focus upon this villain's supposed powers does seem to obliterate your awareness of the Allness of God. This is where limitation sets in and restriction and destruction seem to appear. GOD IS ALL. GOD IS HIS OWN WILL (WAY). GOD'S WILL IS ETERNALLY DONE AS THE ONLY WILL BEING DONE AND THERE IS NONE TO OPPOSE IT. GOD IS ALL.

## In Earth As It Is In Heaven

Of what benefit is it if God's will of perfection and glorious living is done in some far-off heaven reachable only by death? Jesus was trying to teach here the practicality of God. Bills must be paid. There must be evidence of bodily health, or what the world calls "healing." Peace must be evidenced as heavenly environs. Otherwise, all of this spiritual talk is just plain philosophical drivel – an exercise in mental fantasy.

For God to be truly ONE and ALL, there can be no splits, separations or divisions whatsoever. There can be no heaven and earth as separate states of existence and yet God be ALL. Many well-meaning Christians and other religionists hold fast to heaven and earth as being separate. Heaven and earth must be separate, they reason; otherwise, getting to heaven has no particular incentive. "Certainly earth cannot be heaven," they mutter, "or else we're in real trouble."

Forget now about the well-meaning Christians and the religionists who believe whatever it is that they believe, and take a good look at your own beliefs about heaven and earth. Do you believe that earth and heaven are separate locations? Do you believe that they are separate states of consciousness, as many metaphysicians do? Do you believe that they are one and the same? If so, how do you justify the violence, destruction, avariciousness and natural disasters that claim the lives of so many in this heaven on earth? You have heard it said, even from the Master Teacher himself, *"According to your belief is it done unto you."* With that, metaphysicians have attempted to believe as positively as possible that heaven is here on earth. There is a law higher than this law, a law whereby you are no longer victimized even by faulty believing. The law is: *"Ye shall know the truth, and the truth shall make you free."* Hereby, we are no longer concerned with beliefs, belief systems or their consequences. Hereby, we are only concerned with what one knows. Do you see that beliefs are at best tenuous, while knowledge is certainty beyond doubt?

The foregoing questions are now reiterated. Do note your answers to these carefully, but be sure to have first answered them in the preceding paragraph. What you are doing is comparing what you *believe* to be so with what you *know* is so. Do you know that earth and heaven are separate locations? Do you know they are separate states of consciousness, as many metaphysicians do? Do you know that they are one and the same? If so, how do you justify the violence, destruction, avariciousness and natural disasters that claim the lives of so many in this heaven on earth? How do you know? Upon what is this knowledge based? Anything that has been taught to you of God and God's Kingdom from an "outside" source cannot be counted on as knowledge. What if your sources are mistaken? How will you know? Perhaps your certain knowledge is based upon observation. Cannot the eyes be fooled into believing that what isn't *is*, and *vice versa*?

One of the myths that must finally be put to rest is this thing of degrees of consciousness. Far too much is based upon this notion of *degrees* of consciousness. Alongside it is the notion of higher and lower selves. All of this is two-ness, three-ness and separation. None of these theories is based upon the Truth of ONE Presence and ONE Power. You will have to discover via revelation that God is All in order to assign these myths to their final resting place – the grave of nothingness from whence they came.

Heaven and earth have been interpreted respectively as cause and effect. This is nothing to quibble over when we take the time to explore that interpretation to its limit. For in doing so, we discover that we are talking only of God. Imagine that on a table before you are two glasses filled to the brim with water. One glass is labeled "heaven" and the other is labeled "earth." What is the difference between the substance that fills the "heaven" glass and the substance that fills the "earth" glass? None. Now suppose you were to pour out half of the water in each glass and subsequently pour water from the "earth" glass into the water from the "heaven" glass. Would you be able to distinguish the "earth" water from the "heaven" water? No. What is the difference between the substance of each glass? Does not the difference lie only in the *labeling* of the substances? The contents of the glasses are precisely the same substance. In the Old Testament book of Jeremiah we have this Truth revealed: *"Do not I fill heaven and earth? saith the Lord."* If earth and heaven are both filled with the Presence of God, is there any difference at all between the two of them? Heaven and earth, cause and effect will both pass away when it is seen that regardless of the words used, we are talking only of God.

Labels can be quite misleading, simply because we seem to believe more in the label than in the thing labeled. In Genesis 2:19

we are told that *"God formed every beast of the field and every fowl of the air; and brought them unto Adam to see what he would call them: and whatsoever Adam called every living creature, that was the name thereof."* The word "name" means *nature*; therefore, the correct interpretation would be "and whatsoever Adam called every living creature, that was the *nature* thereof." Remember, heaven and earth are filled full with the presence of God, yet Adam attributed a separate nature to each manifestation of God's presence. Essentially, the beasts of the field and the fowl of the air are God and have the nature of God as their *only* nature. Howbeit, lions are ferocious by nature, snakes are venomous by nature, scorpions are stinging by nature, and so on and on down the line of separate and distinct natures. When natures and traits are attributed to the presence of God, the same identity that names them is the same identity that must deal accordingly with the thing as he has named it. Mind, intelligence, knows the lion to be God, knows the snake to be God, knows the scorpion to be God and knows every presence that is present to be God. This same Mind knows earth to be heaven and heaven to be earth. It knows cause to be effect and effect to be cause, thus no time separates them at all. In Isaiah 11:6-9 we are given this prophecy: *"The wolf also shall dwell with the lamb, and the leopard shall lie down with the kid; and the calf and the young lion and the fatling together, and a little child shall lead them. And the cow and the bear shall feed; their young ones shall lie down together; and the lion shall eat straw like the ox. And the sucking child shall play on the hole of the asp, and the weaned child shall put his hand on the cockatrice' den. They shall not hurt, nor destroy in all my holy mountain."* How can they when ALL IS GOD?

Understanding this idea called "cause and effect" is of utmost importance; otherwise we find ourselves wrestling with frantic attempts to demonstrate Truth. All frustration in spiritual practice is a result of these attempts to demonstrate Truth, a carryover from the metaphysical belief system of cause and effect. It is enough to know that, whatever the name applied to *anything*, GOD IS ALL THERE IS.

## Give Us This Day Our Daily Bread

There is much to say regarding this statement. It can be approached from many angles. Again, this prayer must be viewed in the present tense simply because Truth is the ever present NOW. In the form typically given, this particular clause seems to be one of begging and beseeching. However, we must take into consideration the declaration made by God given in Isaiah 65:12: *"Before they call, I will answer."* There is no such thing as God and man, but for the sake of clarification it can be said that before man comes to the point of need, God has already provided the needed thing. This could be wisdom, money, love, food, peace, health and the like. There is a reason why this is so and it will be explained later in this section.

In John 6:32-35 we read these words spoken by Jesus, *"I am the bread of life: he that cometh to me shall never hunger; and he that believeth on me shall never thirst."* *Bread* is anything that assuages man's seeming hunger. *Bread* could be in the form of a home, right employment, companionship, food, furnishings, understanding, peace of mind and so on. Jesus the Christ perceived that the congregation was looking for a key that would give them more *things*, much as we tend to look for the right affirmation or perhaps some mystical formula that would fulfill all our desires. He told them that *He* was the bread, *He* was the formula, *He* was the key, *He* was the answer to total and complete fulfillment. The Christ pointed out to them that they had tasted the bread of flour and meal, they had enjoyed health, companionship and other desirable things, but not one of these was enduring because not one was the TRUE MANIFESTATION of these things. Thereupon, He invited each and every one of them to come to Him that they might not ever experience hunger (unfulfilled desires) again. He had spoken these words before: *"Come unto me, all ye that labour and are heavy laden, and I will give you rest"* (Matthew 11:28). Imagine total surcease from the desperate attempts to attain some desired good! The key was given, but it was so simple that it was not believed to be the *key*. Perhaps like many now, they misunderstood and thought they were to come to a man named Jesus, and that He personally would provide rest and solace. Not so!

Jesus identified Himself as the Father and as Truth Itself. He said He was (and is) the light of the world and further proclaimed that each and every one of us is that very same light. By His testimony He and the Father were one and the same, and He implied that our identity was (is) as His. Certainly we have seemed to believe we were something greatly separated from the Father. But this has never affected our True Identity.

Can you imagine God needing anything? If so, you would never go to God for those things you seem to desire. Whether or not it is from past religious training or what have you, most of us have believed that God had whatever it was we wanted. God not only has everything but IS everything that actually exists. Dear reader, this is the same God that we have for so long called "The Father." It is the same *Father* that you are.

In one sense, when we view the phrase "Give us this day our daily bread" we can recognize it to mean "Give me a full and complete understanding of my *identity* that is all and needs nothing." This understanding is the bread that comes down from heaven, which bread, correctly interpreted, is the manifestation that comes from the conscious awareness of God the Father as the only Presence, Power and Cause; and of your identity *as* this Father.

I am convinced that there is no greater understanding than that of Self-Completeness: the needless Self that never needs to lean on anyone or anything for its supply and support. For he who has this understanding of his identity shall indeed never hunger or thirst again for anything. Why should he? Does God hunger?

Does God thirst? Is there any beside Him? If you cannot answer these questions with any degree of certainty, it is necessary that you ask and ask and ask again until the revelation is imparted.

At one point in His teaching, Jesus made it clear to the Hebrews that the bread Moses provided was not "the true bread from heaven" that, once partaken of by any man, that man would never again hunger. Certainly, the bread that Moses provided did appease the hunger of the Israelites temporarily, yet because it was not the assimilation of the Truth of their Self-Completeness, they continued to hunger. *We will all seem to hunger until we have the revelation of our own Completeness.* Things will not satisfy, except temporarily. One who works toward satisfaction by a continual round of accumulating thing after thing will forever seem unsatisfied. This is the lesson of manifestation by revelation. At the point of your agreement with your own Completeness, you can safely leave the concern about demonstration alone. Henceforth seek total awareness of your Completeness as God. As revelation after revelation streams forth, watch the glorious exhibition that accompanies these revelations.

Our Father, your universal Self, is whole and complete at every point. Revel in this wholeness. Taste it in the silence of your meditations. The knowing of your own Identity is freedom from hunger.

It is wonderful that Christ Jesus has taught the lesson that would free one from the old metaphysical concern of making demonstrations. Here in the contemplation of God's Completeness, *which is your own Completeness*, you can literally watch all the lovely and wonderful "things" flow into your life as evidence of God's Completeness. For example, perhaps you have an empty room that needs furnishing. In the old way, probably you would visualize and mentalize furnishings being added or money being received for their purchase. In the system of the finished Kingdom, you would do nothing of the kind. Instead, you would keep focused daily on your Self-Completeness (God's Completeness) at every point. You would not be thinking of furniture, money or decorator appointments. Soon you would find that somehow the room was furnished. Somehow the project was finished. Somehow a right companion appeared. Somehow a more rewarding job came forth. Somehow incomplete health became complete health. My friend, be clear about the fact that nothing has changed at all. Seeing through a glass darkly (human vision), you perceived an incomplete universe, an incomplete body, an incomplete mind and an incomplete life. Now the blinders have been removed and you see your Self and world as it is, the very glorification of the Completeness of God. *Seek ye first the understanding of your Complete Identity* and all those things necessary to evidence it will be added unto you. Here, it is of utmost importance to understand that you, of yourself, no longer have the luxury of this thing called "human planning." In the full understanding of Completeness, there is nothing to plan. The mad attempts to fulfill some petty human desire indicate that one has not fully comprehended his Completeness. Spiritual logic has revealed to you that desires, all of them, are merely signals to recognize your own Completeness. Safely, you can let go of the notion that you *as a personal identity* must *do something* to fulfill these desires. Desires speak of incompleteness. They speak of nothing. Transcend the desire for things as such and focus on *total* awareness of this word Completeness.

The "bread of life," *which bread you are,* is Life Itself. Moreover, it is eternal Life. *"This is that bread which came down from heaven: not as your fathers did eat manna, and are dead: he that eateth of this bread shall live forever"* (John 6:58). A true understanding of your Identity is the understanding of how to live forever. This is the understanding that is victory over the grave. This is the understanding of how to conquer the last enemy – death itself. This understanding yields the unduplicated feat of Jesus Christ – self revivification. By this lesson demonstrated by Jesus, if a man, *any* man, would feast upon his own Identity, he would live forever.

## Forgive Us Our Debts, As We Forgive Our Debtors

Frequently, you will see this written as *"Forgive us our trespasses, as we forgive those who trespass against us."* Again, it is imperative that this be interpreted in the present tense: "Forgive(s) us our debts as we forgive our debtors." Already you see that this is not a statement of begging and beseeching a far-away God concerning some supposed act of omission or commission.

Within these very lines is contained a lesson on love and judgment. It is a lesson on how to best settle debts and all other unfinished business. According to Paul in his epistle to the Romans, the only debt owed at any time is the debt of love; this debt paid in full is the fulfilling of the Law. *"Owe no man anything, but to love one another: for he that loveth another hath fulfilled the law."* To act as love is to exhibit patience and kindness. It is to bear full witness to Truth. Acting as love is to act free of evil, selfishness, self-importance and evil motivation. "Love never faileth"; for "God is Love."

God *is* Love. God *only* is Love. These things called human beings (which you are *not*) cannot love nor know anything of Love; therefore, they find themselves in a continual state of indebtedness. The qualities of God are not given to nor channeled through human beings. This is impossible. There is none beside God to funnel God through. To truly love is to BE LOVE. To be Love is to BE GOD. Do not make the mistake here of thinking that any amount of "spiritual work" is going to transmute a so-called human being into God. Rather, human beings (as they have seemed to falsely identify themselves) realize themselves *as the very presence of God*.

The debt owed is love; it is paid by seeing beyond the untruth of "separateness" and "otherness" to behold the One in all its resplendent glory. You, my friend, are this One.

Forgiveness is right judgment. Forgiveness is the refusal to judge after the appearances of separation, imperfection, evil, injustice, and the like. Forgiveness is judging righteously. To judge in righteousness is to judge according to the Law of One Presence and One Power. Forgiveness is never fulfilled as long as one perceives "two-ness" and "otherness." If *identities* are perceived, and not the One Identity, there has been no forgiveness.

I can recall a time when I felt I had been rendered a gross injustice by a much-loved friend. In this great fiction, I allowed myself to steep in anger for many days. At length, having grown weary of what I knew to be purely phantasmagoric emotions, I became receptive to seeing exactly what was the case. In my meditation I realized there was no one and nothing to forgive. God Is All, and I (not the fictitious "i") AM that ALL. There is (and was) nothing beside the ONE Identity that I AM. There was never another identity. Be clear about the fact that this has nothing to do with an Allen White of "human" lineage, for he can perceive nothing of the I AM. With this great revelation came an instantaneous experience of harmony, freedom and limitless Love. There was no judgment, for there was nothing and no one to judge. GOD TRULY IS ALL. This revelation was the debt paid in full.

Perhaps at this very moment, it appears as though there is someone who has wronged you terribly. It seems that you are angry, perhaps even bitter. A floodtide of indignation and resentment has you in emotional and physical turmoil – it seems. Love IS the fulfilling of the Spiritual Law here. Believe me, there is no *other* law to fulfill; and the fulfilling of this law is *by recognition only*. The Spiritual Law is simply the omnipresence of God that IS. Right here and now is a good time and place to begin seeing the falsity of the appearance of separate bodies and identities, for certain it is that anger, resentment and unforgiveness are born of the idea of "two-ness" and "otherness." All of these emotions must be directed *at* someone and must originate *with* someone.

Find your favorite spot for meditation or prayer. After settling in, ask your Self: "What is my true relationship with (name of person)? Is there really a relationship at all?" Do not attempt to answer this intellectually. Listen with total openness for the answer to be revealed. It is very important that you continue with this to the point of revelation.

For those who are involved in what are called "personal relationships," it would be most revealing to ask your Self this very same question. Keep in mind that it is *the revealed answer that is power*. Wait joyously and expectantly for the revealed Word on this – and any – question. With the answer will come the automatic dissolution of appearances of discord and inharmony in your "relationship." Also, the answer revealed (and not reasoned) will be sure and certain immunity against the typical upheavals that plague those who are in a relationship with "another."

Yes, it is a fact that all "human" misunderstandings (as they appear) are the result of ignorance concerning the actual relationship between what are perceived as two identities. The liberty to reveal what is Truth here will not be taken in order that you may discover this vital Truth for your Self.

Many who recite the Lord's Prayer misunderstand the line "forgive us our debts as we forgive our debtors" to mean that God forgives us to the degree that we forgive others. Let's take a good look at the absurdity of such an interpretation. First and foremost, this notion involves three identities; thus God is not ALL. Second, man (the created) is ultimately more powerful than God (the creator) in that man's actions alter the nature of God. (This is not to suggest that there is a creator and a created, but those who seem to misunderstand in this way do believe such.) Last, by this, God is no longer seen as the Power and Presence that is Love itself, but rather, a being that has the capacity to love or not love (as do those which are called human beings). Spiritual logic clearly shows that the above interpretation based upon multiple identities is entirely false.

The Holy Bible states that God is of purer eyes than to behold evil, and cannot look upon iniquity. This revelation found in Habakkuk 1:13 is totally contrary to the popular belief that God sees evil and rewards the doers of evil with varying degrees of punishment. God sees no evil. What does God see? GOD IS ALL; therefore, God sees Himself *only*; and this Self is not tainted with evil at all.

At one point the disciple Peter came to Jesus and said, *"Lord, how oft shall my brother sin against me, and I forgive him? till seven times?" Jesus replied, "I say not unto thee, Until seven times; but, Until seventy times seven."* There is much that is significant here. Seventy times seven equals four hundred and ninety. Added together these product digits total thirteen. One plus three equals four. The number four has great spiritual significance. It symbolizes complete awareness of the Allness of God. In Revelations 21:16, John the Revelator speaks of *"the city that lieth foursquare."* Do take the time to read that entire chapter. This city *"had no need of the sun, neither of the moon, to shine in it: for the glory of God did lighten it, and the Lamb is the light thereof.... And there shall in no wise enter into it any thing that defileth, neither whatsoever worketh abomination, or maketh a lie: but they which are written in the Lamb's book of life."* This city is the Consciousness of God manifested. Its purity, by virtue of God's Onlyness, is symbolized by the Lamb which lights the city. In this Consciousness there is not the slightest awareness of impurity, whether that impurity be disease, sadness, incompetence, poverty, violence or any other negative condition. *Only God is seen in this consciousness.* This is the consciousness that is of purer eyes than to behold iniquity. It is seen to be your Consciousness and my Consciousness when there is no more false judgment as to who and what we are.

Jesus' response to Peter had nothing to do with the traditional "I forgive you." Rather, the response was in reference to the Consciousness that continuously and forever gives forth the True judgment of the Allness of God. The judgment of this consciousness does not see thieves and prostitutes. It does not report of publicans and sinners. It has no awareness of black or white, Greek or

Jew, male or female. All is seen to be the sinless purity of God. What Peter did not understand was that this Consciousness was *his* consciousness right at the moment he was asking this question of Jesus. The consciousness of "seventy times seven" is not in an "act" of forgiving, ever. It is simply God judging all as His glorious Self.

Concerning the so-called "act" of forgiving in which human beings supposedly engage themselves, it cannot be done with the effectiveness intended. Have you ever noticed that when you have supposedly forgiven someone of some heinous offense, there still is a knot in the stomach every time you see that person? Have you noticed that each time you are in the company of that person, the offense automatically comes to mind? Have you noticed how often you have told this tale of the supposed wrong-doing to anyone who would listen, since the time you had supposedly forgiven that person? Is this forgiveness? No. It does not require spiritual logic to see the ineffectiveness of this kind of forgiveness. HUMAN BEINGS CANNOT FORGIVE. The true act of forgiving is totally foreign to their nature. In exercising the polluted "act" of forgiveness, humans often have much difficulty because the concept is so far removed from what humans have assessed life, living and God to BE. Let us right now totally dismiss the notion that someone can engage in an act of forgiveness. *"I of myself can do nothing,"* declared Christ Jesus; and this is true of anyone of himself or herself. *"The Father* (Universal I AM) *doeth the works."* God forgives nothing and no one because beside Him there *is* no other. When human identity is put aside and it is clearly seen that *"I and the Father are one,"* there is nothing and no one to forgive. There is no one to cause knots in the stomach. There are no emotional ties to memories of hurt and pain. There are no folktales about the "someone who done me wrong." All of these are completely dispelled. What would you give for God to be seen as the ALL of ALL? Would you willingly give up the belief that you exist separate and apart from the Allness, the

Power, the Glory, the Majesty of God? For the appearances of humanhood, would you give the Truth that beside God there is no other, not even yourself as a personal identity? *This* is forgiveness.

## Lead Us Not Into Temptation But Deliver Us From Evil

What kind of loving God and all powerful God would allow his "children" to be led into temptation of any sort, or would allow them to experience even the slightest degree of evil? To think that we have to beg a loving and powerful God to lead us not into temptation seems ludicrous from the start. We can safely assume that this line means something quite opposite to the accepted belief of the masses.

*Immediately!* Right now! Be done with the begging stance and the futuristic tone that this line seems to suggest and read it in the present tense, the NOW tense: "Leads us not into temptation but delivers us from evil." Does this not seem more fitting of a God that is Love and Omnipotent? However, there is still much to discern here. To think that God leads us and delivers us is to think in terms of *two*. This is blasphemy, since we do know that GOD IS ONE, and the ONLY ONE. God is ONE; therefore, who is being led and who is being delivered? No ONE. What is meant by this line? Much.

In Psalm 23, David exulted, *"The Lord is my shepherd, I shall not want. He maketh me to lie down in green pastures: He leadeth me beside the still waters.... He leadeth me in the paths of righteousness for His name's sake."* The Lord is the Spiritual Law, the Law of *"...the Lord is God, and there is none else."* This Spiritual Law negates the laws of nature, the laws of aging, decaying and death, the laws of economy, the laws of genetics, and all other restrictive and degenerative laws that are not laws at all.

In the desperate attempt to describe God, certain words employed have been accepted as true and fact. You are quite familiar with some of these words in their "spiritual" context –

Love, Omniscience, Mind, Intelligence, Life, Substance, Omnipotence, Omnipresence, Consciousness and so on. God described as Mind is God fully aware of His Presence present everywhere as the All *in* All *of* All *as* All. There is not one iota missing or absent from this awareness of Himself. This is Mind in action. Since God is Omnipresent Mind, these questions must be asked: *Who has a mind that is not this Mind? Can I have a mind that is not this Mind and God still be All and Omnipresent?* The answers to these questions are important and must be revealed so that the spiritual significance of this section of "The Lord's Prayer" can be perceived.

The Lord that makes me to lie down in green pastures, that leads me beside still waters, that restores my soul is the Law of One Mind. Can you imagine God being tempted by the appearances of evil to believe that evil is a reality in His omnipresence? Can you imagine even for one moment that God is at all tempted to believe in lack, in turbulent upheavals between "personal" identities, in a "valley of the shadow of death"? With what mind then are you and I seeming to believe this insanity? The correct interpretation of this line is: "When I know that I have no mind of my own except the omnipresent Divine Mind, I am no longer tempted to believe that there is a presence and power outside or other than the One Presence and Power that is God."

*"Let no man say when he is tempted, I am tempted of God: for God cannot be tempted with evil, neither tempteth he any man. But every man is tempted, when he is drawn away of his own lust, and enticed"* (James 1:13-14). This is utter Truth. Temptation has absolutely nothing to do with God. Why? There is nothing other than the Allness that IS GOD to tempt *with*, nor is there *anything* or *anyone* to tempt. However, man does seem to be tempted by *something*, and that *something* is his own desire to *have* something, *do* something, *be* something of his own single and separate identity. The appearances of evil and temptation will seem to go on *ad infinitum* until man ceases believing himself to be something other than God Itself. As long as man sees himself as a separate little

something, there will always be something *outside* and *other* than himself. He will forever be tempted to love or hate, like or dislike this "other" person, condition or thing. Whichever be the case, he has established some attachment to this "other." This is the start of temptation. If man likes this *other* thing, he will use all of his "personal" resources to merge with it. He has been tempted thus to believe in separation and incompletion. If he hates this *other* thing, he will entertain the false notion of being threatened by it; thus he believes in negative powers, hatred, and separation.

When man beholds his I AM identity, there is nothing beside; nothing to love, nothing to hate and nothing to be tempted by. The notion of temptation and the realization of one's identity cannot exist simultaneously.

Man can neither be tempted nor tested by God. Orthodoxy would somehow have man believe that God uses disease, destruction and disaster to test his faith. If God cannot behold evil and wickedness, and does not know anything about them, how can He use that of which He is ignorant as a measuring rod? Moreover, this assumption is based upon the idea of God *and* man. Somehow, reader, you must discover the Truth of the Singleness and Allness of God. Many of the seeming trials and tribulations that you have deduced to be "testings" by God will automatically vanish into their native nothingness when you realize what is so.

The realization of One Mind is the deliverance not only from the appearances of evil, but from the belief in evil as well. Many well-meaning Truth "students" have entertained the false notion that Truth is to be used *against* evil. Knowingly or unknowingly, their basis is that evil is the reality, and that there must be some formula (physical or metaphysical) that would lessen the power and influence of evil. This is discovered to be pure nonsense when One Mind is realized. Automatically, thoughts take a new direction. There is no attempt to control the thoughts; like magic, they tend to focus on that which is lovely, that which is Truth, that which is joyous and of good report. Initially, this may not be the case all the time, but as one contemplates the idea of One Mind and new realizations stream forth, negative thinking takes a seat further and further back until there is no place in your conscious awareness for it at all. It is then that you can proclaim, *"Mine eyes* (spiritual perception) *have seen the glory of the coming* (Presence) *of the Lord* (Spiritual Law). *"* And surely this Truth is marching on as the only activity and power there is and ever was.

The realization of One Mind is the realization that evil is not a presence, power or entity at all to be dealt with in any way. Truth is not power over evil. Truth does not dispel evil nor deliver from evil. It has no dealings with evil simply because it has no awareness of evil. Disease, nuclear destruction, death, violence, abuse, lack, sin and turmoil – all of which are evil's malicious offspring – are left in the valley of nothingness when Truth is seen as All. Ecstatically, the Psalmist shouted, *"Yea, though I walk through the valley of the shadow of death, I will fear no evil: for thou art with me."* Digging to the core of this proclamation, we discover that upon walking through the valley of the death of joy, the death of success, the death of love, the death of plenty, the death of happiness, and so on – all of which are the shadows of nothingness – one certainly does not fear at all. One knows that God Is All and that God's Allness is not only with him, but is his very presence. Hallelujah! It is easy to understand David's jubilance when he perceived that evil was not a power to fight against. The majority of humans spend a great part of their lives fighting against one form of evil or another; and if they are not actively fighting *against* a present form of evil, they are engaged in a process to *prevent* evil. *Is this living?*

Frequently, sincere ministers of metaphysical religions urge their congregations to "let go of evil." They go on to tell them that evil has no power, yet they follow this statement with warnings of the power of negative thinking. Have you found it difficult to *let go* of evil? Have you found it difficult to *stop fighting* evil? Certainly anyone who believes himself to be anything less than God will find both difficult. And certainly anyone who thinks he has a mind and "free will" of his own will find both difficult. God *and only God* has no dealings with evil. Only the Mind that is God knows no evil. Apart from this Mind there is *nothing*. *Nothing* includes sickness, old age, poverty, death, despair, frustration, and so on. Each and every being inherently knows the Truth. *This* Truth that he knows is his freedom.

## Thine Is The Kingdom, And The Power, And The Glory, Forever.

There is tremendous power in the understanding of this statement of Truth. This is not just "the tail end" of the Lord's Prayer. Rather, this clause carries within itself a profound message of Truth.

In the progression from orthodox religious practices to metaphysics there still remains one carryover that has been the undoing of both, and that is the use of God, Truth, to better a human body, identity and world. The devout practitioners of both orthodoxy and metaphysics cannot deny that Truth has *not* been the major focus of their concern. Things, tangible and intangible, have been the main focus. Prayer has been used to improve marriages, obtain money, acquire homes and automobiles, enhance the physical appearance, gain a sense of peace, afford elaborate vacations, purchase furnishings, and the like. It does seem that prayer has been helpful even when misunderstood and "mis-applied." All of this prayer activity has been based upon some degree of lack. Moreover, it has been based upon a misconception of the identity of the one who prays. Nothing of any great value can come of anything having a foundation steeped in such falsity.

The Kingdom of God, which is in fact the Kingdom of heaven, is God and God's. God is the sole inhabitant of His Kingdom. There is not a man, woman, child, grasshopper, weed, flower, and so forth in the Kingdom of God. Right at this very moment you may be puzzled by this statement, but do read on. The foregoing statement being true, it seems paradoxical that the Kingdom is at hand, is omnipresent, is right now, just as Christ Jesus taught. Perhaps you have agreed, if not acquiesced, to the fact that the Kingdom *is* at hand. And certainly you have felt no reluctance in admitting that the Kingdom is eternal and omnipresent. But it is right here at this point of admitting that the Kingdom does *not* include men, women and children that you draw the line. However, it is this very line you are drawing right here that hides the Kingdom from your vision and experience. Coming into the Kingdom (the *awareness* of the *already* present Kingdom) requires that you shed the garments of humanity at the door. It requires that you forget all human history and identity. This means all human failures and successes, all human hatreds and loves, all human acts of omission and commission. There is no room in the Kingdom for any of these. The Kingdom is already complete and ripe for the harvest. Everything necessary is there, and this obviates the need for a human being coping with the vicissitudes of human living. What seems to blind us from the sighting of the Kingdom is the desire to *add something else* to it. God fills full His Kingdom. Only God sees His Kingdom. No man will ever see or experience it because it is nowhere near him. Howbeit, you *do* dwell in the Kingdom – but not as man, woman or child nor as offspring or images of another. You, beloved, dwell in the Kingdom as the very presence (a focal point) of God. If this were not so, God would not be All. The statement of Jeremiah the prophet which reads, *"Do not I fill heaven and earth? saith the Lord,"* would be a lie.

If a glass is filled with water – really filled – is there room for ice? Is there space in that glass for even one drop of another substance? The earth and heaven are filled to capacity with the presence of God. Where is there room for man, woman, child, bird or bee? If any form is in the Kingdom, *it is God formed*. These forms can be mistakenly identified as *anything*, but that does not alter the fact that the form is God. GOD IS ALL. ALL IS GOD. The understanding of this is the sighting and the experience of the Kingdom of God.

Why doesn't Truth work? Have you ever asked your Self that question? Surely in periods of seeming dismay and despair you have asked yourself this question; but the fictitious self that you have asked can no more give you the answer than it can "make Truth work." Do you fully understand – and you must, given who you are – that any attempt to *make* Truth work is a vain attempt to glorify a false sense of human identity? Truth *cannot* and *will not* glorify this identity, for it *knows* nothing of it. All attempts by this identity to get Truth to *do* something for it will meet with failure and frustration.

Until God is given all honor, all glory, all majesty, and *all identity*, it will seem as though Truth is not working. It will seem as though time is necessary for Truth to work. What the one who attempts to "use" Truth fails to notice is that the time it takes for it to "work" is endless. The only thing working at all in these instances is the faith of the one who is hoping that Truth will someday work. God is Truth. Do you believe that God is having a problem with God? To God, Truth (God) is working and has *always* worked. No, this is not work to *change* anything. This is purely the joyous activity of Being.

*"I am come that they might have life, and that they might have it more abundantly"* (John 10:10). Yes, the Christ identity which is God *identified as all* has indeed come – that True Life might be experienced. Human beings, regardless how hopeful, will never experience this Life. This is the Life that is God. It is the Life lived only by God in His omnipresent Kingdom. When the realization of who and what manner of being you are "comes," then you will live, and live only because it is God living His own life. Perhaps at first you experience this intermittently, but once having had the experience, you will undoubtedly have it again. This is the life lived not by human might but by the

power and presence of omnipotent God. *"Not by* (personal) *might, nor by* (personal) *power, but by my spirit, saith the Lord of Hosts"* (Zechariah 4:6). Already you sense that this is not a life of strain and struggle, not a life speckled with misery and pain and suffering, not a life of boredom and drudgery. This is the abundant life of Christ.

ALL IS GOD and GOD IS ALL. All of the statements of pure Truth that you have ever read, heard or spoken are statements in testimony of the Life and Presence of God. They have absolutely nothing to do with the life and presence of that which we call "man." Life is testimony to Itself. Life is the glory of Itself. Life is God. All is to the glory of God. "Thine is the glory" is a statement of pure Truth. What else could be glorified? Does it bother you at all that in True Living you will have no glory at all – of yourself? This question must be answered from the heart. If all of your so-called "study" of Truth has been for personal glory, you will continue to look for new "formulas" that work – but which never really work. Nothing can give you the satisfaction you seek but the discovery of your omnipresent Glory – that Glory which is not exclusively focused in any one place, but is everywhere equally majestic and beautiful. Does it bother you that your neighbor, your friend, even that which you have called your enemy, will be found to be equally glorious in the Light of Truth? Again, this too must be answered from the heart, simply because *they* will be perceived to be as wonderful as you perceive *yourself* to be.

*"Verily, verily, I say unto you, Except a corn of wheat fall into the ground and die, it abideth alone; but if it die, it bringeth forth much fruit"* (John 12:24). Truth is not an antidote and preservative for human life. What is called human life is no life at all. There cannot possibly be a God in a life so chock-full of misery, disappointment, failure, fear, distress and limitation. Did you perhaps think that eventually God would banish these evils from life? What has taken your god and your truth so long in eradicating

these gross appearances from your world? Could not an omnipotent God instantly eliminate even Satan himself? Yet, it is the belief of many that God allows Satan and evil to chase, catch and destroy creations that are in His very own image and likeness. As Jesus stated, it is essential that you fall into the ground and die in order to bear spiritual fruit. "Falling into the ground" is merely the full and total recognition that GOD IS ALL and there is no other identity beside. Having realized this fundamental Truth, it is impossible for you to live as a human being any longer. You must be God Life personified.

The only way to praise God is to glorify God; and the only way to glorify God is to BE God. Again, this is not to be misunderstood as an elevation of the human to the Divine. This will never happen. Many people take immediate offense at this statement of being God. They falsely assume they are to believe that this sick, aging, miserable, powerless being they have identified as themselves is God. To the contrary. This identity is no longer to be found when God is truly known to be ALL, ALL, ALL. Do not take the phrase GOD IS ALL lightly. Ask your Self what is the full meaning of these words. The revelation will clarify many of your questions.

It cannot be said too often that certain words need to be spiritually defined – particularly those words that are used to describe God. One such word is "power." Certainly you have claimed God to be all-powerful or all power. Perhaps through "spiritual exercises" you have even claimed your own power as your Divine inheritance. Have you taken the time to consider wisely what you have been saying? Is God to you all power and therefore can swiftly vanquish all forms of evil? Is omnipotence power *over* something? How often have you associated the power of God with the overcoming of some line of resistance? Have you claimed power as your Divine inheritance to bolster your confidence in coping with the evils of human living? Is God in the perpetual business of fighting evil?

God cannot behold (see) evil; therefore, it would be impossible for God to even attempt to fight it. *"With God all things are possible,"* declared Jesus the Christ; but this has nothing to do with battling the myriad appearances of evil. Power as seen in the eyes of the Divine is simply *the ability to do*. It is the ability to do all things smoothly, efficiently, successfully, economically, creatively and perfectly. When the omnipotence that is God is rightly perceived, it is cognized as the Supreme ability to do all things. It is just as easy for God to maintain the planets in their orbits as it is to bloom as the flowers in spring. The omnipotence of God knows no levels of difficulty. As a focal point of the Presence of God, you have no "personal" power *over or against* anyone or anything. God is not aware of anyone or anything other than His single Presence. Realizing yourself to be a focal point of power is the recognition of your (but not of yourself) ability to do all things smoothly, efficiently, successfully, economically, creatively, easily. The power is still God's. It does not belong to the focal point because the focal point is nothing in and of itself. The glory for all accomplishment belongs to omnipotence Itself. ALL IS GOD AND GOD'S.

Our Father, which art the Cause of all that has being,

Whole and Perfect is Thy Nature, and the nature of All existence.

Thy Kingdom of Love, Joy and Peace has come upon the earth. Thy will of Perfection now governs this earth. By virtue of Thine omnipresence, heaven and earth are now indistinguishable.

Thine all-sustaining Presence crowns my life with the fullness of Thine omnipresent being. I want for nothing.

As we are seen "in Thine image and likeness" (a focalization of Thine omnipresence), so we hold every man, woman and child in Thy perfect likeness.

In and as the omnipresence of Divine Mind, I am not tempted to believe in aught but Thee. I am delivered from the appearances and effects of seeming evil.

In Thee I am glorified, in Thee I have all power. The Kingdom of my life is Thine omnipresence.

# CHAPTER THREE

# Conscious Awareness

Alice Ross recently lost her husband to another woman. Her children are ill and her live-in sister has a drug addiction. Unemployed and without income, Alice will soon lose her home. The stress of all this has made Alice look fifteen years older than her well-lived forty-one years. What can the beleaguered young woman do? Pray, of course.

It seems that prayer is the suggested remedy for all of life's extremities. Prayer is supposed to be a sort of magic wand whose sole function is to transform the discords of human living. Sometimes it works and sometimes it doesn't. If those who pray and those who have prayed would be candid, they would admit that prayer is not all that it is claimed to be. First, there is the confusion about how to pray and to whom to pray. Then there is the delay that always accompanies prayer – *if* it is answered. Finally, too large a percentage of prayers *aren't* answered, or they are not answered in the way we would *like* for them to be answered. Human prayers are just as hit-or-miss as is human life. Everything associated with human beingness is based upon uncertainty – prayers included. It may seem somewhat blasphemous to call prayer (the most touted of spiritual tools) haphazard, but read further, my friend. What is being said here is that *human* prayer, not prayer *itself*, is highly overrated. This is probably due to the fact that prayer is used as a "spiritual tool." Tools are always used to fix something. Prayer, as humans have used it, is always in the business of adjusting some body, situation or thing. It is always in the business of acquiring somebody or something. It is always in the business of restoration. Where GOD IS ALL, where is there need for such a tool? Is God in a state of disrepair? Is God in need of restoring? Is God in need of fixing? Then what is the purpose of your prayers? If you answer, as many do, "To bring about the kingdom on earth," then God is not all. It is time to take a look at what it is that we do believe. And as always, our speech and actions betray us.

How *does* one pray? If we were to follow the advice of Paul and "Pray without ceasing," we would not have ample time to even greet our neighbor, nor would we be able to hold down jobs, attend to household duties, eat, and so forth. The only other possibility is that somehow we have been mistaken about what prayer really *is*. Perhaps in the right understanding of prayer, we would hold down more rewarding jobs, greet our neighbor with the courtesy and respect he or she deserves, and attend to other duties more efficiently and effectively. What is prayer to you? Is it a means to an end, or the end itself? If it is a means to an end, what is that end – more goods of this world?

Many questions arise concerning prayer. Among those frequently asked are: What is prayer? How does one pray? What is the difference between prayer, meditation and contemplation? How long and how often should one pray? Whom does one pray to – Jesus Christ or God? Is it legitimate to pray for anything? Are affirmations really prayers?

Some of the nonsense about prayer can be immediately dispensed with once we gain a perspective on prayer. Let us return now to Alice Ross. Using prayer in the traditional sense, Alice would probably begin to automatically prioritize her petitions to God. Loving her husband the way she does, certainly she would ask God to return him to her. The children are also important, so of course she must ask God to heal their bodily diseases. Financially depleted, Alice would surely pray for employment and money. Bear in mind that the stress of her circumstances has aged her considerably. Therefore it is quite possible that she would, through prayer, seek a restoration of her youthful beauty and vitality. If all of these prayers were "answered," would it not encourage Alice to believe that prayer is a tool usable to adjust the empty and half-filled spaces of her human life? At some point she would want a bigger and better home, new furnishings, companionship, clothes, vacations and other "finer things of life." Alice would undoubtedly utilize prayer to obtain these and more. When would the lust to have more, do more and be more ever end? It would *not*. The law of human experience is absence and vacuity. The human mind does not know anything of being – only of *becoming*. Therefore, human beings always entertain a sense of "something missing." They forever hunger and thirst for some person, place, condition or thing.

It is strange how these beings persevere in setting goals, achieving them, and then go on to set new goals. Yet these beings are never satisfied. It seems they would understand that the satisfying of their own lusts is not the key to that Satisfaction that never again lusts: The Satisfaction that *"...shall be in him a well of living water springing up into eternal life"* in the finished Kingdom. Prayer based upon acquisition is falsely based prayer. It must always come to naught.

Acquisition has no place in the Kingdom. God is not in the business of acquiring or becoming anything. An account is given in the Bible of a time when Jesus entered a temple in Jerusalem and observed the selling of oxen, sheep and doves and the activities of the money changers. It is recorded: *"And when he had made a scourge of small cords, he drove them all out of the temple, and the sheep, and the oxen... and overthrew the tables; And said... 'Take these things hence; make not my Father's house an house of merchandise'"* (John 2:15-16). The *house* is the consciousness. This is where man dwells. Rightly seen, the Consciousness is God. Wrongly seen, often even by the most devout metaphysicians, it is a tool for acquisition. It thinks and conjures up schemes to feed its lusts. In the false sense of "elevation," it holds positive thoughts and even employs the word "God" for the purpose of manifesting the object of its lust. However, with the entrance of Light and Understanding of the Self, these "tables" of schemes and thoughts of acquiring and becoming are "over-turned." In the finished Kingdom, where dwells the Christ that you are, there is no concern with *getting* or *becoming*. The tables of acquisition are turned over by the force of revelation that I AM is in need of no thing.

It is plain then that prayer is not a tool for acquisition or for the improvement of a "material" world. Another mistaken notion that can be immediately dispensed with is that prayer is the endless recitation of statements of Truth. Jesus told His followers, *"...when ye pray, use not vain repetitions, as the heathen do; for they think that they shall be heard for their much speaking... for your Father knoweth what things ye have need of, before ye ask him"* (Matthew 6:7-8).

Any bird capable of speaking can learn to speak the words, "I am human." Though he were to repeat this throughout his entire life span he would never take on the appearance or capabilities of a human being, simply because he has no concept at all of what it is or means to be human. Similarly, a human being can declare over and over, "I am God," and never evidence anything of a Divine nature, simply because he (as a human being) has no idea of what it is or means to be Divine. However, he would by appearances move into his human idea of God. This sounds marvelous, but a human idea of God no matter how lofty is only that – an *idea* of God. It is not God.

Are the metaphysicians who employ countless affirmations attempting to convince themselves of the veracity of their statements? If so, it will never work. If the statement is of Truth, a human mind will never be totally convinced of it. If the affirmation is not of Truth, but merely a positive statement of the "personal" ability *to have, do or be* something in the world as it appears, it is not prayer because prayer is of God and Spirit, not of matter and man. Oftentimes it seems that those who enjoy the use of affirmations do so because it gives the mind something positive to do. The practice of Truth does not involve physical or mental battle against the negatives of human life. The human must initially "stand still" both physically and mentally. This seems hard to those who continue to identify themselves as human. They determine that if they really stand still and do *nothing*, nothing will be done. The basic premise is that *something* needs to be done. This is not the premise of Spirit, whose beneficent *"Come unto Me"* invites every man to rest from his labors. Having mustered up enough faith to stand *physically* still, these affirmers of Truth find the demand to stand *mentally* still too difficult. So they fool themselves into thinking that they are "working with Truth" by engaging the human mind in statements of Truth. They will get as far in their endeavors as will the parrot who affirms he is human.

*"Therefore take ye no thought...."* Jesus realized a tremendous truth and hence proclaimed that one who recognizes who and what he is cannot add one cubit to his identity by the process of thought-taking. He knew that one who has realized exactly who and what this *world* really is cannot add to it one cubit of satisfaction or completion by thought-taking. Furthermore, that same one would see that there is no need whatsoever for anything to *be* added. Thoughts are not power. GOD ALONE IS POWER and there is absolutely no power beside. *"...In such an hour as ye think not, the Son of man cometh."* Beloved, do understand this to mean that as long as you are attempting to create, build or attain Christhood, you are in the very process of denying your *already* Christ Identity. In that moment when you forsake the attempt to mentally

create heaven and mentally create an elevated self-image, you will discover that you are presently *already* the Christ.

There are those who reason that affirmations plant seeds of Truth in the subconscious mind which then grow to manifest that which has been affirmed. Surely, by now, this line of reasoning seems silly to you. It assumes that there are "levels" of Mind. Mind knows no levels, no degrees. Mind is God equally present as the All of All. The whole business of levels seems to outpicture as the *haves* and *have nots*. Injustice, cruelty, poverty, ugliness and ignorance have their base in the fiction of *levels*. Let us dispense with this foolishness right now. There are no levels. Furthermore, this assumption casts man in the role of co-creator – as if God is not already the forever present finished Kingdom – as if God needs the aid of man. Look at that which man has wrought. If God needs man's help, man is in no need of God. Blasphemous as this statement may sound, it requires contemplation and revelation.

Among affirmation adherents are those who may choose not to use *one* statement over and over, but choose instead to rehearse a *series* of Truth statements – as if they need to convince God that they have been faithful in their understanding and memorization of Truth. It would seem that in their meditations they seek to remind God of some Truth that He may have forgotten. According to the doctrine of Christ Jesus, all repetition is the activity of heathens.

If prayer is *not* a coming before God with a host of requests to patch up a human life, and it is *not* a recitation of statements of Truth, it must be concluded that prayer has little or nothing to do with "talking to God," which is often the case. In Ecclesiastes 5:1 we are advised, *"Keep thy foot when thou goest to the house of God* (prayer)*, and be more ready to hear, than to give the sacrifice of fools: for they consider not that they do evil. Be not rash with thy mouth, and let not thine heart be hasty to utter any thing before God... therefore let thy words be few."*

There is the mistaken notion held that if one sits silently in the expectation of "hearing" God, his life will not be practically affected. Surely, nothing will change by true prayer; however, the one praying will discover that *nothing needs to be changed*. One with a sick and palsied body will delight in the discovery that the entire appearance was that of the illusory substance of dreams, and that his body has forever been whole, radiant and vibrantly alive. One who has seemed to suffer great pain will discover through Revelation that pain has never occupied a place in the omnipresence of God's glory. He who presently finds himself impoverished, limited and a victim of repeated injustices will revel in the Holy Annunciation that the fields of plenty, peace, joy, love and freedom are ripe for the harvest *right now*. There need be no more months of delay in fulfillment when all the while God is All as All. The grander discovery is that the shackles of humanhood have vanished in the Revelation that he who has seemed to suffer for so many years needlessly *has always been* the free, unrestricted "light of the world."

You must understand that to persist in the practice of "talking to God" is to persist in a false assumption of separation. Already God is not All. This premise is not the solid rock of Truth. Rather, this premise is shifting sand. One must consequently sink into further disappointment and despair and must join "the assembly of the dead." Moreover, the language of man is foreign to God. God knows nothing or no one in need of help. God cannot behold iniquity or evil, neither can he look upon these. How then can God destroy that which he cannot see or is not even aware of? When man comes begging and pleading about first one problem and then another *ad infinitum* he is talking to *himself*. Perhaps there is comfort to be found somewhere in this practice; however, it is not a spiritual practice. How can God be convinced that a universe totally filled by His omnipresence is lacking anything, is diseased "by" anything, is affected by that which does not exist? The revelation always comes to those who listen: *"Beside Me there is no other."* Why therefore bring human testimony into the courts of the Lord? Human testimony is always false simply because there are no human beings. The only being there is, is God Being. Man in his mis-identification cannot give to God a perspective of his universe, which is God's very own Being. It cannot be done. It is therefore necessary that man sit still in prayer "more ready to hear." What he hears is the Divine testimony of the universe and all therein. What he experiences is Revelation. Revelation is the bread of life, the living waters whereby man need never suffer death of anything – body, supply, peace, happiness or wealth.

Having taken a close look at this begging and pleading type of prayer, in retrospect you will recall times when this type of prayer seemed to be answered, and ultimately to your dismay. Perhaps it was a specific mate that you wanted to be "yours." Somehow it came to pass and it was the worst relationship you could possibly become involved in. It may have been a specific job that you simply *had* to have. You prayed long and hard about it. Suddenly the position opened to you. However, the stress and politics involved were more than you could conceivably endure. Your subsequent prayers were about getting *out* of that position. Paul knew the fallacy of this kind of prayer and said, *"For we know not what we should pray for as we ought."* James, who is described as a servant of God, expands on this with, *"Ye lust* (after things) *and have not: ye kill, and desire to have, and cannot obtain: ye fight and war, yet ye have not, because ye ask not. Ye ask and receive not, because ye ask amiss..."* (James 4:2-3). Paul and James both agree that praying folks don't seem to know exactly what to pray for; therefore, even their "answered" prayers leave them with a sense of emptiness and sorrow.

The basic premise of Truth, no, the *only* premise of Truth is GOD IS ALL. Therefore, if any man seems to lack anything – money, home, companionship, employment, health, love, peace, joy – what he really lacks is God. Of course, he does not *really* lack God because God is all there is of him. What he does seem to lack is a *full awareness* of the ALLNESS, ONLYNESS AND ISNESS OF GOD. Therefore, what he needs to pray for, if praying for anything can be legitimatized, is revelation of God's Presence. Solomon called this "wisdom and understanding," and proclaimed that having this, one would have everything necessary to live a full, glorious and majestic life, all to the glory of God's omnipresence. To pray for anything else is to admit that God is not enough. It is an acknowledgment of something other than God. This is a flawed premise and man cannot possibly find any fulfillment whatsoever in pursuing this line of thinking. If the premise is false, all the thinking, doing and being will be false. If one could possibly take an aerial view of the lives of those who mistakenly think them-selves human and God afar off, he would discover that their activ-ities are no more fruitful than those of a hamster spinning around in his cage getting absolutely nowhere fast.

Wisdom and Understanding – Spiritual Wisdom and Spiritual Understanding – are the seeming need. Solomon knew the impor-tance of spiritual wisdom and spiritual understanding in the attain-ment of the heart's true desire: *"Wisdom is the principal thing; therefore get wisdom: and with all thy getting get understanding"* (Proverbs 4:7). He knew that with this wisdom and understanding would come total life satisfaction. Was he himself not proof of the factual practicality of wisdom and understanding? Is there any-thing else to understand but God? Is not God Spirit? It is this false assumption of humankind that there is something else to under-stand other than God that has led many off into foreign realms of discovery. However, all their discovery has failed to yield true and total life satisfaction. Why? Because what they have discovered is *nothingness*. Certainly it seems that this nothingness masquerades as different *things*, but the fact remains that if it is not knowledge and wisdom of God, it is knowledge of *nothing at all*. The dis-covery of nothing yields nothing. One may argue of the many dis-coveries in the medical field. But what have they yielded? Disease still runs rampant and death is still the last enemy to overcome.

Has there been any true satisfaction in the discoveries of "materia medica"?

How are you to obtain spiritual wisdom and understanding? The first answer to this question is the *wanting* of it: *"If thou seekest her as silver, and searchest for her as for hid treasure; then shalt thou... find knowledge of God"* (Proverbs 2:4-5). This, however, is not enough. If you are going to look for anything and find it, you must look for it where it is located. Spiritual wisdom and understanding are not to be found anywhere in the human mind. All searching for the Great Something in the nothingness of the human mind will be futile indeed. True prayer is effected when all sense of the human mind is completely obliterated and the Divine Mind shows forth as the Actual Mind of the one praying. With this experience come wisdom and understanding. The one praying must yield himself up to this experience by the refusal to hold onto a fictitious identity and a mythological mind. Christ Jesus said, *"When thou prayest, enter into thy closet, and when thou hast shut thy door, pray to thy Father which is in secret; and thy Father which seeth in secret shall reward thee openly"* (Matthew 6:16). Have you really considered the meaning of this helpful prayer hint? To fully understand what the Master is saying here is of tremendous importance.

Jesus often spoke in symbolic language and this passage is a classic example. Although some choose to literally enter into a closet when they pray, this is neither necessary nor enough. In the "closet" of true prayer, one is isolated from the world. The incessant demands of the world are not here. The destructive powers and influences are not here. The sense and appearance of emptiness and dissatisfaction are not here. The pictures of poverty, violence and desolation are not here. Wants, needs and lusts are not here. They are in the world, but they are not in the closet of true prayer. The closet is the Kingdom of God. Anyone who prays therein prays truly, and savors the finished Kingdom of God present in all its perfection.

Those who seek to *witness* the Kingdom and not *create* the Kingdom, pray truly. Those who have no desire other than the direct experience of God, pray truly. Those who seek first and exclusively the Kingdom of God and its righteousness, pray truly. This, the sole desire to witness what IS, is entering into the closet. In the Kingdom there is no room for humans nor human concerns. Those must be left at the Gate of Nothingness from whence they came. No one who attempts to "use" prayer for the attainment of things and the elevation of the human self has ever truly prayed at all.

Many associate "entering the closet" with darkness. This is good. In total darkness there is nothing (no thing) to see, want or experience. God can be said to be the Great NO THING. God has no awareness of any "thing" at all other than His Allness. God sees no "thing," hears no "thing," experiences no "thing" and creates no "thing." God IS, and there is none beside. It is in the darkness of not seeing things to desire and lust after, to heal and cure, to multiply and restore, that the Light of God is seen and experienced.

It is often said that this type of prayer is impractical and does not yield the experience of God. So it would seem. No one who holds himself as a human being will experience God. There must be a willingness to let go of this false assumption to experience the effectiveness of this type of prayer. Moreover, there must be a willingness to discover that you are *presently* God in order to have what has been called a "God experience." Only God witnesses God. Closing the Gate of Nothingness behind you, you must be willing to shed the garments of humanness. All it takes is the willingness. Everything else will automatically be taken care of in the pure intent to "see" God. SEEING IS BEING.

Does God desire anything? Any prayer based on *things* is not prayer at all. Do understand that the experience, the revelation, the knowing is actual prayer. The process is not prayer at all. It does not matter what you do *activity-wise* that leads to this experience that you are indeed the God Presence you have been seeking all these many years. When Paul exhorted us to *"Pray without ceasing,"* he meant that it is necessary for everyone to eventually experience uninterrupted, constant and unending God awareness. Is this possible? It is what you have been seeking all the while. True and lasting satisfaction will never be attained until this occurs.

Initially, it seems that God is far-off or distant. Although metaphysicians have proclaimed God to be within them, they have still managed to convey the concept of dimensional space and distance. How deep within is God? The metaphysicians will have no greater experience of God than the traditional religionists, simply because there is still God *and* themselves as separate entities. This seeming distance is *"the Father which is in secret."* When the one praying is fully open to the experience, this same secret Father rewards that one with the open revelation that *"the Father and I* (pray-er) *are one* (and the same).*"*

The open reward is the experience of ineffable peace and joy, unfailing prosperity and abundance, abiding love and companionship, eternal health and wholeness, and total satisfaction in life *now*, during this "earthly" walk. All of this is the result of realizing that "I and the Father are one," and *there is no separation* at all.

Perhaps you are thinking at this point, "Well, what about things – money, homes, cars, positions, mates and clothes? How do I get these things? What formula do I use? Did not Jesus say, *"Ask and it shall be given unto you, seek, and ye shall find; knock, and it shall be opened unto you: For everyone that asketh receiveth; and he that seeketh findeth; and to him that knocketh, it shall be opened"*?

Yes, these are the exact words of Jesus the Christ recorded in Matthew 7:7-8. However, preceding this the Master made it absolutely clear *what* was to be sought and found: *"But seek ye first the kingdom of God, and his righteousness; and all these things shall be added unto you. "* Yes, all who seek the Kingdom will find the Kingdom. All who ask for the Kingdom will be given the Kingdom, and all who persistently knock for it will have the doors of the Kingdom flung wide open to them, that their joy might be full to overflowing. Believest thou this?

Do you believe that, in finding the Kingdom of God to be now at hand, the host of needs you have seemed to entertain (when you thought you were a human being) will automatically be satisfied and not only satisfied but *immensely* satisfied? Or do you believe that something still must be done either physically or mentally to establish the Kingdom? Do you really believe that any human effort at all will bring you the satisfaction that seems to be missing from your life? Has your human effort brought you satisfaction thus far – *real* satisfaction, not of the temporal variety? Do you not seem to still hunger for that special *something* that would fill the seeming void in your life? How, then, could it be at all possible that effort along the lines of human beingness will bring you anything other than what it has hitherto brought you? Jesus knew the futility of trying to establish and accomplish anything of oneself, while laboring under a false assessment of oneself as human. This is why he was able to say, *"Seek ye first the kingdom of God...."* He knew that the Kingdom was *now, presently at hand*; and that anyone who sought it exclusively would find it because it has been here all the time. Jesus knew also that only God inhabited the Kingdom of God and therefore any man who found it would necessarily find himself to be the very Presence of God. How wonderful this must be! How wonderful it *is*.

It is here in the Kingdom of God – in the Consciousness of God – that man accomplishes much but works little. Here the "sweat of the brow" method of attainment is null and void. Here man has come into the knowing that HE PRESENTLY IS THE CHRIST and rests from his labors. The heavy burdens of futility, frustration, disappointment and despair have fallen away by weight of their own nothingness. Here man reaps where he has not

sown. Ecstatic life satisfaction is his. This awareness is prayer –
TRUE PRAYER.

Let us not be unduly preoccupied with the length of time it
will take to come into the conscious awareness that GOD IS ALL,
that the Kingdom is at hand, that the field of satisfying living is
already ripe for the harvest. To be too preoccupied with this question is to deny your present Christhood, and the end result is contrary to the hoped-for Revelation. Yet be not deceived. Upon the
recognition (that initial perception that precedes Knowingness)
that GOD IS ALL, that the Kingdom is at hand, that the fields are
*right now* ripe for harvest, it is of utmost importance that you seek
greater awareness of *that which you know in your heart of hearts
to be true and Truth*. This perception is the "Angel of God" come
before you. It bears the message that you and your life are not
what they appear to be at all. It speaks to you of the majestic quality of your MIND, BODY and LIFE, now at hand.

It was at night when Jacob was alone near the ford Jabbok
that the angel (of awareness that there is something greater) visit-
ed him. He did not ignore the angel, nor did he deal casually with
the angel. Jacob knew in his heart that the angel had something
specifically for him. Therefore he wrestled with the angel
throughout the night, and in the heat of the fight proclaimed: *"I
will not let thee go, except thou bless me."* And Jacob was certainly blessed. *"For I have seen God face to face,"* he proclaimed.
(Genesis 32:22-30). Everyone has sensed that there must be something more to life. Man has often, in quiet moments, sensed his
own greatness. After having perceived this and even enjoyed the
experience for a fleeting moment, he has gone on with the busyness of being human.

This was not the way of Jacob and it must not be your way.
Every spiritual perception that flits across the mind must be
attended to with the sure knowing that a blessing follows. Not a
blessing in the sense that something can be added to your already
present perfection, but a blessing in conscious awareness –

beyond the intellect – that where you stand presently is Holy Ground, that the body with which you move is Holy Substance, that the mind you have identified with is Holy Consciousness. This is the blessing that is given when one seeks greater awareness of those truths he has intellectually perceived.

Are you willing to stay up all night awaiting revelation, or is this something that is done in your spare time? Jacob was so enthralled by the Truth that he knew was revealing itself that he was mindless of passing minutes and hours. Are you willing – not out of discipline but out of a thirst and love for Revelation – to forget about that favorite television program, that weekly meeting, the bowling league, and any other present attachment, for the sake of Revelation? There will come a time when it will be a joy for you to set aside all those things that had formerly been important to you, just to sit silently as Revelation streams forth within and as your very own being. What a joyful time this is. It is written in the Gospel of Luke that Jesus was once found in the mountain praying to God and that he continued in prayer all night. This was not disciplined behavior; rather, this was behavior born out of the love for Truth.

The disciples were fascinated by the Nazarene who claimed to be the Son of God. They believed Him and believed *in* Him as the Son of God. At one point, the disciples asked Jesus specifically about prayer, and requested: *"Lord, teach us to pray, as John also taught his disciples."* Jesus responded with one statement of Truth after another. These statements combined are now known as "The Lord's Prayer." No longer is there the man Jesus to teach us anything; but there *is* the Christ, the True identity of each and every one of us. It is this same Christ identity that is the Comforter who will lead every so-called human being into the full awareness of who and what he is and *always has been*. Just as the disciples approached Jesus with this request, so can you address your Self with this very same request: "Lord of my being, teach me to pray."

There are many books, ministers and lecturers that profess to have the key to effectual prayer, yet none has come forth with a "method" that has been universally satisfactory. None will. Prayer *as a state of constant awareness of the Allness of God eternally present* is every man's natural state of awareness, clouded though it may be with the mistaken sense of ignorance. Prayer as a tool to come in to this awareness *cannot be taught as a universal method*. Each man must come into the Revelation of *Isness* in his own way. The reason for this is far beyond the scope and purpose of this writing. However, it is necessary for each one to discover his own way. The quickest route to this discovery is simply by asking Christ (your Self), "Lord (of my being), teach me to pray." As always, what is more important here is not the asking but the sitting still and listening for the answer. Noticeably, some things are repeated again and again. This is done purposely. What cannot be too often repeated is: Guard against the tendency to intellectualize or reason out the answers to your questions. You will know when an answer you have sought has come. You will have a feeling of total satisfaction, as opposed to the restless dissatisfaction that often follows answers that are reasoned out from the *no mind*.

# CHAPTER FOUR

# Answers

This section is presented in response to questions asked the author.

Do not consider any of the answers as the final revelation for you. In the event you should find a particular answer disconcerting, do not immediately discount that answer; instead, ask your Self the very same question and let your Self reveal the answer. Do this in totally open consciousness.

## What is the best position in which to meditate, contemplate or pray? Is there a particular posture that facilitates spiritual growth and revelation of God?

Many so-called gurus and "enlightened" individuals would have you believe that there is some magic formula, position or posture that would promote spiritual awareness. There is no such formula or posture. What is that posture which seems most comfortable to you? What is that position which gives you a sense of "open" consciousness? That is your posture at any given time. It may not conform to anything that your friends or other "enlightened" ones are doing, but what is that to you?

Again, there is no posture that will facilitate spiritual growth. To believe otherwise is to start from a false premise of Self. You are the finished splendor of the Self. It is true that something may spark your awareness of this fact, but it never changes you, not even for the better. Does God need changing? Is there any beside God? If this seems hard to grasp and you cannot start from the premise of your Perfect Identity, then it is better that you not start from any premise at all. This way you are in a position to behold your Self, divorced from any and all false conceptions.

## What is the quickest road to riches and wealth?

There is no "quick road" to riches and wealth. It is true that many people have come into metaphysical religions hoping to find the answer to their money problems, but the answer is not found in Truth – not by way of formula, nor things to do and say.

Acquisition is the much traveled road of humanity and human beings. Everything and everybody seems to be seeking to fulfill some void, some sense of emptiness. They (human beings) have thought that God would be the answer to the incessant demands of their lust to have, do and be.

Do you believe that God is lacking anything? Do you believe that God has money problems – bill problems and credit problems? Do you think that God is busy trying to attain anything? If so, who or what would give to God that which God craves? Is God All? It would be wise to ask these questions of your Self. The revelation is wealth in itself.

Dear reader, most human beings have expended a great deal of mental, physical and emotional energy in the quest for more and more money. (Their labors have not rewarded them in kind.) Now, let's suppose that wealth and riches were redefined to mean the True knowledge of your Identity, the True knowledge of God and the True knowledge of the Universe. Let's suppose further that the same energy was expended toward Revelation of these truths. What do you think would be the end result? God, of course.

God, who has no need. God, who is not struggling to attain anything. God, who has no credit trouble. God, who is not concerned about dollars and budgets. This is true satisfaction – the satisfaction that every human being seeks. However, it will not be found in human beingness. Are you human? Is God All? Is God human?

Our Bible states that with the understanding and wisdom as to who and what we are comes wealth, peace and eternal life.

## Do thoughts and words have power?

This question takes its rise from the history of metaphysics, wherein thoughts and words were used in healing the mind and body of various discords and diseases. If you were to trace the development of the New Thought movement beginning with Mesmer to the establishment of the three major metaphysical branches, you would see where this false notion has its roots.

No, thoughts and words do not have power. God and *God alone* is power. God has no power – but God IS power. GOD IS ALL. All the Power that is, is God being that Power. *God* and *Power* are synonymous terms. They both *are the same thing.*

There is nothing that a human being can think or say that has any degree of power *whatsoever*. God is not human. Every being that has misperceived himself or herself as human is really God. When man realizes this, he has no need for his thoughts or words to have power. He sees as God sees. This is vision that cannot behold iniquity, evil, disease, destruction, sin, sorrow or shame.

Metaphysicians have used the Bible passage, "So shall my word be that goeth forth out of my mouth: it shall not return unto me void, but it shall accomplish that which I please, and it shall prosper in the thing whereto I sent it," to justify their attempts to create happiness and prosperity by the "power" of thoughts and words. However, they have ignored the opening passage of the first chapter of St. John: *"In the beginning was the Word, and the Word was with God, and the Word was God."* To understand the former passage, the latter must be considered. Correctly interpreted, the

Word that goes forth is the *very presence of God* in its complete splendor. It cannot return void of anything because it is the Eternal Everything. God will always exhibit success because there is nothing to oppose God, the All.

Negative thinking cannot affect omnipresent Perfection. Why be concerned with negative thinking at all? The human mind will always think negatively. If this is your concern, it is necessary for you to realize that God as Mind is the Mind that you are. Ask your Self what the nature of your mind is. Do not be content until the answer is revealed. Be willing to BE the Mind that is God.

## How can I best help friends and family members who are diseased, distressed and otherwise limited? What magic words do I say? Is there a formula that would help all who ask me to pray for them?

Wouldn't it be absolutely wonderful if there were indeed some special affirmation or formula that, if repeated an "X" number of times, would heal our families, friends and loved ones of all the diseases and limitations they seem to experience? Would it not be absolutely wonderful if we could instantaneously help all those who seem to be suffering?

It is fascinating that not a single book of the metaphysical variety has issued such a formula. Moreover, the various so-called formulas many employ that seem to work at one point no longer produce the same results at a later time.

To have this question answered satisfactorily, *you* must first answer a question or two. When family, friends and loved ones come to you diseased, distressed and otherwise limited, do you believe the picture they portray enough to sympathize and empathize with them? Is God diseased, distressed and otherwise limited? Is the picture of their neediness a *true* picture? Why, then, need you bother at all with that which is not true? No matter what comes before you, no matter how distressing the picture appears or sounds, it has nothing to do with the Truth that GOD IS ALL.

Now, my friend, when this revelation announces itself, the appearances of disease, distress and limitation are discovered to have never been there at all. This shows forth as what the world has called "healing"; however, *you* know that nothing has changed at all.

Again, your only concern is for greater revelation of Allness. Here's a hint: This revelation will be slow in coming forth if there is any attempt at all to behold Allness as something separate from your very own being. *"Let this mind be in you, which was also in Christ Jesus. Who, being in the form of God, thought it not robbery to be equal with God..."* (Philippians 2:5-6).

## I must work every day. Then too, there are many things that I must attend to at home. How can I pray, as Paul says, without ceasing?

If you are thinking of prayer as an act, as something that must be performed in a particular way, at a particular place, this cannot possibly be done.

Prayer is the Conscious Awareness of the ALLNESS OF GOD. It is the Conscious Awareness that your identity is God – not an image (for an image is nothing) and not a likeness, but the very Presence of God. Is this sacrilegious? No. How else will God be All unless you are that Allness Itself? Where does God leave off and you begin? That is the very place where God is not All. From this standpoint one is no longer dealing in Truth.

Allow yourself to behold your Self as *who* and *what* you really are. The question is now, "Can this awareness be maintained for any length of time?" The continued, uninterrupted experience of this Awareness is "the prayer without ceasing."

The other question contained within this question is, "How do I find time to behold who and what I am?"

I do not know what it is specifically that you must do other than the simple willingness to BE who you are. But whatever it is, if beholding your Self is important to you, you will find time to do what seems necessary – just as you have found time to do household chores and those activities associated with your employment. We always find time for that which is important to us. How important is it to behold that you are now free from every sense of limitation that is associated with this phantasmagorical human scene?

## When praying, do we pray to God or to Jesus? Are God and Jesus the same?

The following quotations from the Holy Bible have given rise to the great controversy as to the who's and how's of prayer:

*"And whatsoever ye shall ask in my name, that will I do, that the Father may be glorified in the Son."*

*"If ye shall ask any thing in my name, I will do it."*

*"...No man cometh unto the Father, but by me."*

Herein it appears as though Jesus is setting himself up as an intermediary between God and man. Already the seeming dualism of the last statement is unsettling – a sure indication that this long-held assumption is incorrect.

Name, of course, means *nature*. Whenever Jesus speaks of "In my name," you must interpret it to mean "In my nature." What is the Christ Jesus nature? Here in the Gospel of St. John, Jesus reveals His nature: *"I and my Father are one (and the same)."* *"He that hath seen me hath seen the Father...."* Christ and God are one and the same. To do anything in the name, or nature, of Jesus Christ is to do it in full recognition of one's own Identity as the full Presence of God. There must come a point where one immediately associates the word or name "God" with his very own identity.

If Christ and God are one and the same, to whom does Christ pray? Christ prays "to" no one or no thing. Prayer, then, is the full Awareness of your God Identity as your only Identity. The awareness is indeed the prayer. No longer entertain the pagan concept of praying "to" God. All prayer "to" God is idolatry.

## If you could recommend one book of Truth, what would it be?

Let's examine this question fully. What are books of Truth? Even our beloved Bible is a composite of individual experiences of God and their revelations. Why should you place more value on the revelations of another than on your very own? The one book I would recommend for you is the inscription of Truth upon the pages of your own soul. My friend, I am speaking of your own *direct experience of your Identity*. Nothing else will ever satisfy.

Please do not misunderstand this to mean that one is not to read spiritual literature at all. What is important is the manner in which you approach your reading. If you think that perhaps you will learn something by reading, you are absolutely mistaken. However, if you read merely for inspiration, and not instruction, you will always be led back to your Self for everything that you seem to need to know. Spiritual parasitism – living off "another's" revelations – is denial of your very own Identity.

## How does one effectively deal with overcoming seeming separation from God?

This is a most frequently asked question, particularly of those who have done away with the husks of metaphysics and have embraced Absolute Monism. Don't make such a big issue of this question. The answer is too simple.

How does one deal with having three heads? How does one deal with giving birth to human typewriters? How does one deal with fighting a lunar war? One doesn't deal with them at all. They are such farcical concepts – not likely to occur – that one does not even consider the idea of "dealing" with them. The idea of separation from God falls into the category of the above. It has never happened. It is not *going* to happen. So why "deal" with it at all?

Instead, deal with One Presence, deal with One Power, deal with Christhood, deal with Omnipresence, deal with Universal

Identity, deal with God *only*. Any other dealings are counterfeit. They render no reward whatsoever.

How can one overcome that which has not happened, and is not going to happen? This is your answer regarding how to deal with the overcoming of seeming separation.

## How can I have those fantastic spiritual experiences I read about so often in various books?

The desire to duplicate the spiritual experiences of another only for the sake of the experience always results in disappointment.

The anxious desire to "have" a spiritual experience is no more pure in motive than to seek God for money, companionship and success. The experience is always the added thing that comes with Revelation of Truth. It is so important to remember that a human being will never have a True spiritual experience. To *have* a Spiritual Experience is to *be* that very experience. Objective experiences are usually psychic in nature. They are as valueless as human experiences.

In direct answer to this question: These fantastic experiences will be yours when you forsake entirely the notion that you are a human being with a human history living in a human/material world.

## In Truth, what is said about alternative lifestyles?

Nothing could be more alternative than *human living*, which is no life at all. All the variations on the theme of human living are variations on "a lie from the beginning."

God is the only Life and the only Lifestyle. Who or what is there to live alternatively?

In the realm of human living and human beingness there is a need for moral codes. There are an infinite number of separate beings who must be externally controlled. This is not so where God is seen to be All there is. There is nothing or no one to judge.

This is not liberty and license to just do *anything*. One who perceives Life as it is cannot act contrary to Life. This one finds that *"the government is upon His shoulders."* There is no need for outside restraint, no need for outside approval. Behavior that is not in accordance with Life itself is neither contemplated, nor enacted. Can Venus of its own accord usurp the orbit of Saturn? Neither can God act contrary to God's own nature.

## Is it necessary to go to church? Does church have any value whatsoever?

The answer to this question is given in Revelation 21:22: *"And I saw no temple therein: for the Lord God Almighty and the Lamb are the temple of it."* Herein, John the Revelator is foretelling the appearance of the Holy City, the New Jerusalem. Jerusalem, the New Jerusalem, is the Christ manifested. More than that, it is the Universal Christ manifested. Do not be mistaken concerning this. This is not a *future* self, a *future* consciousness or a *future* manifestation. It is the *present* Self, the *present* Consciousness and the *present* manifestation.

The Universal Christ manifested has no need for churches and temples as they appear presently in "this world." Here monuments, from the starkly simple to the ornately grand, are erected to teach beings who are presumed lacking in knowledge. Even if it is knowledge of each individual's own divinity that is taught, these institutions operate under the assumption that there is someone lacking in wisdom. They, the churches, attempt to fill this void with "spiritual wisdom." Well, this is impossible. If these institutions had spiritual wisdom as their foundation, they could not possibly operate from a void-filling premise.

Traditional churches and temples are not much different in their approach. They propose to somehow convince man that his actions and attitudes need adjusting in order to be pleasing to God. They operate from a sense of dualism that is astounding. Both the metaphysical and traditional churches are founded upon the attaining of some goal in the near, distant or perhaps never-to-come future. They view man as being sorely in need of redemption. The churches claim to offer salvation, yet they seem inexorably entrenched in the low (and false) esteem in which they hold mankind. The redemption offered is not possible. If man is a sinner by nature, if he is a worm of the dust by nature, his nature *will not* and *cannot* change. Can a cat become a horse? Can a fish bark? Neither will a sinner be righteous. It is not his nature. No amount of praying will make a sinner righteous.

Do not think that I am against churches. Rather, I propose that the church change its stance from one of redemption and salvation to one of celebration – that the church be a place where people come of their own choosing to celebrate for an hour or so their already present-and-operative Divinity. As soon as the minister proposes to teach, educate, change or heal a single member of the congregation, he is already on the shaky grounds of dualism. All churches and ministers operating in this manner must go. They serve no useful purpose whatsoever.

Attend church as you would a good lecture. Be absolutely clear that you are in need of no instruction, no redemption and no salvation. GOD IS ALL. Let your measuring rod for every book you read, every lecture you hear and every church you attend be: "Is this the doctrine of the Allness of God?" If so, revel in your "Our Father" (universal) identity and have a good time. If not, it would be wiser to close the book, leave the lecture or walk out of the church.

## How does one manifest the Allness and Perfection of God?

This question has plagued mankind throughout the ages. It has been disguised in various forms such as: "When will I find fulfillment and satisfaction? When will my ship come in? When will I be free from this turmoil?" Anyone who has ever voiced these or similar questions has denied the manifest Kingdom (Consciousness) of God now at hand.

There is a metaphysical law that holds true even in the Absolute: "As in the mind, so in the experience." However, we state it somewhat differently: "As in Mind, so in the experience." In metaphysics there is the belief that the individual mind manifests according to the quality of thoughts held in that mind. This of course is not true. What *is* true is that omnipresent Mind is its own omnipresent manifestation. Christ Jesus calls this "heaven at hand." His confirming words to us are, *"Say not ye, There are yet four months, and then cometh harvest* (fulfillment)*? behold, I say unto you, Lift up your eyes, and look on the fields; for they are white already to harvest"* (John 4:35).

Needless to say, the Vision of Spiritual Perception that is focused on the debris and desolation of the human experience cannot expect to see the Kingdom *now at hand*. The perception must be allowed to soar above disease, death, destruction, violence, hatred, poverty and human beingness. Nothing will be found in the human world, for it is nothingness itself. The Great Something that all have longed and hoped for will be found in the ALLNESS that IS GOD. This question is now answered. The nothingness of human beingness cannot manifest the Something of God's Allness. The manifestation of God's Allness is of no concern to God. God knows that only God is now manifest. To see the Kingdom of Satisfaction one must know that one is God Himself. Any attempt to manifest satisfaction is not the activity of God. It must end in disappointment and frustration. The Kingdom cannot be denied and manifested simultaneously. The Truth that GOD IS ALL cannot be acknowledged and denied simultaneously. To declare yourself as one working diligently with metaphysics to manifest the Kingdom is an outright denial that God IS ALL.

One *does not* and *cannot* manifest that which is *already fully manifest.*

## If God is all there is, and all there is of anyone or anything, how did evil enter into the picture?

If you have ever entertained this question, I ask you to ask yourself this very same question now, omitting the word "how": "If God is all there is, and all there is of *anyone* or *anything*, DID evil ever enter into the picture?" The Bible, of course, attempts to answer this question in its opening chapters of Genesis.

To search and search for the answer to this question requires that the searcher first believe that *the evil really is here*. He cannot possibly reconcile the appearance of evil with his belief that GOD IS ALL, because he *does not believe* GOD IS ALL. It is impossible to act contrary to one's belief. It *is* possible, however, to act contrary to what you would like to believe is true. To have this question answered with any degree of satisfaction, I urge you to ask your Self, "Is God all?" and "Does evil exist?" It is supremely important that you keep at these questions until they are revealed within and as your very own consciousness. Again, I urge that you abandon the idea that something is going to be revealed "to" you. This idea will only serve to delay the experience of revelation. The revelation is *your very own* Consciousness. What's more, it is your very own experience.

## How can I use Truth to attain and maintain a healthy body?

Truth will not seem to be evident and presently manifest to anyone who is seeking to "use" Truth for selfish purposes, regardless of how noble and righteous the purposes may seem.

To "use" Truth automatically implies that Truth (GOD IS ALL) is not presently and completely manifest. The second and more ghastly implication is that there is *someone* or *something* other than the Allness of God. In this posit one has placed the omnipresent Kingdom of God at a distance farther than the remotest star.

Health means wholeness. The Lord's Prayer speaks of health as being the nature of God: *"Hallowed* (whole) *be Thy name* (nature). "* Wholeness or health is indeed the nature of God and is the nature *of God only.* It is *not* the nature of that which is called man. It is the nature of man to be devoid of wholeness and health. To evidence perfect health, it is necessary to identify yourself as that which is health, God. *"Let this mind be in you, which was also in Christ Jesus, who being in the form of God, thought it not robbery to be equal with God...."* Let that Mind reveal itself to be your Mind revealing the comforting message that thou art, yes, *you,* the living Presence of God *right now.* It is then you will *know that you know* that wholeness – health – is the inviolable nature of your being.

Health is not attained, neither is it gained or earned by diet and exercise. Health is recognized to be an integral fact of this vast, vast universe which is the *present* omnipresence of God. Anyone trying to "get" health has already established in his or her mind that it is presently separate from him or her. The greater the effort to attain it, the more it is affirmed to be presently absent. Forsaking this notion of human identity will reveal health right where it is: Here. YOU.

## Why am I here?

Perhaps you, reader, have asked this question many times. Usually it is precipitated by thwarted goals and a pervading sense of futility. There seems to be a point in one's life when it appears quite obvious that the dreams of success, fortune, love and the "good life" formerly entertained will never be realized. Sunk in the mire of human living, one begins to question the why's and how's of it all: "Why am I here?" "Is this (human life) a mean joke that God takes great pleasure in projecting?" "How can I escape?" These and many more questions begin to surface.

Dear friend, if you have ever asked these questions of your self, I would urge you to ask *this* question of your Self: "Am I here?" So often we ask questions assuming that the basic premise of our questioning is real – is reality itself. The question "Why am I here?" is really asking "Why am I here in human (restricted) form, with a human (limited and debilitating) life in which success, prosperity, love and happiness are against the normal pattern of existence?" Further thoughts along this line center on aging, illness and the steady march toward the grave. It seems to the questioner that life is a capricious path fraught with endless hurdles. It seems that one is beaten before the race begins. Take heart: NONE OF THIS IS REAL.

The question that must be asked and answered is, "Am I here as a human being with a human life filled with obstacles to overcome and hurdles to jump? Am I here of myself?" Always this question is preceded by an acute sense of individual existence, and an overwhelming sense of separation from everything. The joyous revelation that you are not here at all will be followed by shouts of glad and joyous Hosannas as you go forth with the triumphant Jesus Christ assertions: *"I of myself am nothing." "He that hath seen me hath seen the Father." "I am the way, the truth, and the life."*

Having no personal life leaves one with no personal responsibility. This is true freedom. The child skips along in joyous abandon, mindless of any sense of personal responsibility. He is free. As an adult, he takes on responsibilities not his own. He smiles less and skips hardly ever. The responsibilities of earning a living, clothing the body, putting food on the table, raising children, maintaining a healthy body, securing supply and finding and sustaining love are a tremendous burden to him because they were never his at all to assume. "Thou shalt not steal" *rightly understood* means that one should not take personal responsibility for any of the foregoing from that which is Universal Responsibility or Divine Responsibility. It also means one should not take Identity from Identity.

GOD IS ALL. God is not confronted with obstacles or hurdles of any nature – and beside God there is none else.

## I try with great effort to be rid of my lower self and live exclusively in my higher self. How can this be accomplished most effectively?

Problems always seem to occur when we start from the premise of two-ness and separation. The most devout religionists will proclaim that "God is the answer," yet in their belief, God is so removed from them that they find themselves drowning in a pool of problems and no solutions within reach.

Metaphysicians have created still another phantom based upon this same old theme of separation. This time the variation takes a different twist – one of a parted self. What could be more confusing than self-imposed (by belief) schizophrenia?

Does God have two selves? Is God all? First and foremost, one must abandon the false belief of *two selves*. The so-called "lower self" is the supposed human ego. It appears real because most people have identified it as their *real self* for the majority of their lives. This makes the so-called "lower self" difficult to abandon totally, so these well-meaning metaphysicians invented a parted self – one higher and one lower. Now, it is this higher self that has been correctly identified as the God Self. What needs to be seen here is that the higher Self is indeed the *only* Self. Once this is perceived, the baseness of the fictitious lower self will be seen dissolving in its own nothingness – quickly or slowly according to the degree of perception that there is only ONE Self, the Universal God Self.

Needless to say, one already – right now – lives as his God Self totally. The appearances seem very much to the contrary, but we are not going to be fooled by appearances. It is imperative that we judge from the standard of God, the One Self as ALL.

The questioner states that it is with great effort that she attempts to live in the higher self. The great effort is there only because of the even greater belief in the parted self theory. Do realize that it is impossible to live in this Self unless one lives AS this Self. Anything short of living AS this Self is a vain and fruit-less attempt to bring imperfection into the realm of perfection. GOD IS ALL.

## Why am I here on earth?

This too is an often asked question. Before reading any fur-ther, it is essential that you note the answer to the earlier question, "Why am I here?"

It has been mentioned that metaphysics has invented its own brand of devil, that devil being the idea of a parted and divided self. In addition, it has concocted a theory of planes of conscious-ness. Some say there are seven progressive planes, with the last being that of pure spirit. Always, reader, it is necessary to measure the veracity of what you read by one rod: "Is what I am reading or hearing holding true to the fact that GOD IS ALL?"

Divine Mind is another name for God. We say God is univer-sal or omnipresent MIND – MIND IS ALL. Be honest with your-self. Do you really believe there are varying degrees of God, where one is more (or less) God than another? Or, do you believe that God is equally God throughout God's omnipresence? God is ALL as that which has been labeled heaven, and ALL as that which has been labeled earth. God is not more God as heaven than as earth.

Thanks to theology, earth has been misrepresented as an accursed place inhabited by sinners and filled with sin and imper-fection. Metaphysics has not been much better in its claim that earth is a learning place to prepare one for proper behavior on some other plane of existence. In each case, heaven is someplace away from self. This is not in keeping with the good news of Jesus Christ that *heaven is at hand.* Yes, even while in what has been called an earthly experience, heaven is at hand, heaven is *now* and now visibly present. What then, has been the problem? The prob-lem has been (so it seems) that while in the nowness of heaven, we have been proclaiming it "earth." We have been proclaiming it an accursed place of injustices and inharmonies. We have been, with great pride, proclaiming it to be a learning institution preparing us for a distant time and place of fulfillment and enjoyment – "According to your belief is it done unto you."

God's will is done on earth as it is in heaven simply because that which has been called earth is God just as that which has been called heaven is God. Right now you probably are thinking, "But if that is so, why does earth seem so unlike what I imagine heaven to be?" This, my friend, is because we seem to insist upon judging after what *appears* to be instead of according to the Golden Rule that GOD IS ALL. A new vision of earth will be your experience once God's Allness is fully accepted as Truth.

In concluding the answer to this question, reference must be made to a greatly mistaken notion. Many people seem to actually believe that the world of form is something "less than" because it can be seen. So accustomed are they to the idea of an invisible God that anything that can be cognized with the senses is judged as ungodly. Spirit or Spirit in form *is the same Spirit*, and the properties of Spirit remain unchanged. If heaven is perceived as invisible Spirit, then earth is visible Spirit; yet it is the same Spirit. *"I change not"* (Malachi 3:6). No one is here on earth. GOD IS ALL. All who are here are here as the very Presence of God, In God and As God.

## What is my purpose in being?

As well as questioning *Why am I here?* and W*hy am I here on earth?* people often ask, *What is my purpose?* There are so many questions within this one question, but probably anyone who has asked this question is mostly concerned about (1) the reason for existence and (2) the specific role he or she plays in this reason for existence.

To answer this question as briefly as possible, let's begin with this Truth: You of yourself, or even as God, have absolutely no purpose to fulfill by existing. You exist because God exists, and

God has no "reason" for existing and certainly no purpose. Whose purpose would God be fulfilling by existing, being that there is no other? To maintain that God has a purpose is to imply there is a void, a vacuum or an emptiness. That vacuum, void or emptiness would have to be God Himself. God would then be incomplete. Who or what else exists that could fill that void? There is no void whatsoever. Therefore, there is no purpose. All purpose and mission are based upon some notion of lack.

Seemingly there are many people who think they have a God-given mission to save the earth, the planet or the souls of sinners. As noble as their efforts are, by appearances they seem to be doing little or no good. Statistics need not be quoted; simply pick up a newspaper every day for one week.

Would God need the help of man to save that which He purportedly created? Furthermore, would God need or perpetuate the paltry efforts of man to save that which He created? Of course not. However, those who are on a self-appointed mission do enjoy a sense of purpose. In many instances, fulfilling that purpose brings on varying degrees of martyrdom. This inevitably occurs because the assumed mission is not based upon the Golden Rule: GOD IS ALL. This Truth heeded, no saving mission or sense of purpose is ever contemplated.

It may seem disheartening to suddenly discover that you have absolutely no purpose for existence, no God-given mission to fulfill. Take heart! The good news of purposeless being brings with it untold freedom and great happiness. Let's explore this further.

It was apparent that the Hebrew family collectively had great expectations of the Messiah when He arrived. Christ Jesus, however, was not fooled. He proclaimed His only "purpose" thus: *"To this end was I born, and for this cause came I into the world, that I should bear witness unto the truth"* (John 18:37). Let's not be duped here into thinking that Jesus was proclaiming a purpose in the sense of filling a void; for at another point we find Him proclaiming, *"I am the way, the truth and the life."* It is easy to see that essentially Jesus was saying, "My purpose is to be my Self, because my Self is all that I AM." To *be* Truth is not something you become; it is your present nature of beingness. To BE your Self is to BE Joy, BE Love, BE Peace, BE Wholeness, BE Life and BE Perfection. A dear friend once wrote a book titled, *Just Be Yourself.* In a nutshell, it speaks of recognizing God and only God to be ALL of your Self. This is not a purpose. This is who you ARE.

How does this translate, for example, into career and job roles, into prosperity and so forth? You can be sure that it does; however, none of these can be the focus of your expectations or realizations. They are automatic results of the expanded awareness of who and what you are. Knowing that you are unhindered Being is the open sesame to limitless opportunities. This knowledge of limitless Being comes only through revelation. This revelation is your Self knowing your Self. Your Self knows only boundless existence and therefore manifests such trust as what the world calls "wonderful opportunities."

Dear reader, do not be concerned at all with your mode of expression. This would only serve to focalize attention on a limited being with the attempt to benefit it with limitless existence. It cannot and will not work. Let the Mind ever cognize the Universal Boundless Self, and all manner of satisfying expression shall be correspondingly revealed and manifested.

## Does fasting heighten spirituality?

Spirituality is Spirit Being Itself. It is Spirit aware of itself, and only Spirit *is* aware of itself. Spirit being itself and being All cannot be heightened; neither can it be influenced in any way by the external performances of man.

Can man better come to know his true identity by fasting? I would hasten to say here that if one has a strong and abiding belief that fasting or any other activity will "heighten" his awareness, it will appear as if this is indeed the case. It is not the activity in and of itself that does anything; rather, it is one's belief that causes him to open and behold his identity. It could just as easily be counting pennies, if the belief is so placed.

As stated, nothing adjusts the unvarying action of Spirit in any way; and yet, one beholding himself to be Spirit finds his activities automatically adjusted. Fasting then may very well be a natural result of right identification. In many traditional religious circles, certain activities are restricted in order to enforce saintly behavior. Somehow, their adherents believe that this adjusted behavior is more pleasing to God. Beware, reader! The basic premise here is an outside God separate and apart from man, a God which man must placate in order to win His favor. This is *not* your God. This is no God at all. Activity – or the absence of a particular activity – does not enhance spiritual beingness. Spiritual beingness does modify, eliminate or elevate individual activity to conform with its nature. For example, love cannot act unlovingly. Anyone who perceives himself to BE LOVE cannot injure his neighbor, cannot hate, cannot commit an act of violence and cannot act coldly or calculatingly. One does not strive to act lovingly. Knowing who he is, he automatically acts accordingly.

To believe that the monitoring or elimination of certain activities causes a heightened degree of spirituality is to believe in "cause and effect." This perpetuates the belief in time, which promotes the belief in spaces, which inevitably yield a belief in separation. One cannot hold onto any idea of separation and behold the fullness of God.

## Often, I see a haze of light around people and objects. Does this have any particular spiritual significance?

Seeing auras (a haze of light around objects) is an experience many people have these days. Unfortunately, few who have the experience understand exactly what is taking place. They have mistakenly thought that they were seeing a field of light around a body or around an object, as if the material appearance of the body or object were the reality. The truth is that these illumined ones were beginning to see the actual body (whether that be a so-called human body or the body of an object). Paying more attention to this vision will at some point result in seeing the entire body as Light.

# CHAPTER FIVE

# And Christ Said...

## "What God Hath Joined Together, Let No Man Put Asunder"

This passage from Matthew 19:6 has been quoted so frequently in marriage ceremonies that its meaning has been falsely identified with the joining of bodies and identities together in wedded bliss. Needless to say, God has no concern with the marital happiness of men and women joined together in legal ceremonies. This sounds too harsh to be true; however, it is here that we must ask ourselves: "Is God the One Presence? God being One Presence, can there be room for others joining together in holy matrimony? If God is all there is of both identities, are they not already joined together? Could they be any more joined together than being the very same Presence that is God?"

In Matthew 22:30 it is written, *"For in the resurrection they neither marry, nor are given in marriage...."* The *resurrection* is symbolic of true understanding and true perception. Through perceiving God to be ALL THERE IS comes the understanding that there is none to marry or be given in marriage.

It seems fitting here to clarify the frequently used statement, GOD IS ALL. If you seem to be wrestling with this, trying to reconcile GOD IS ALL with the innumerable appearances of separate identities and things, STOP! Instead of interpreting this statement of Truth, GOD IS ALL, to mean God is everything, take it to mean exactly what it does mean: GOD IS AND THAT'S ALL THAT IS. This keeps the focus away from things, situations and bodies to heal and repair. As this Truth is clarified for you, there will be less and less concern with appearances.

The question remains, "What has God joined together if not man and woman?" The answer is "Nothing." God being the One Presence, there is nothing left to be joined together. However, there is great significance in this statement of Jesus. Man, seeming for so long to imagine and believe that he is a thing apart from God has devised various schemes (both theological and metaphysical) to get *back* or *near* to God. In thought and belief, he has seemed to "put asunder" the Truth that he is presently, *right now,* God – completely and fully God. It seems that he (man) has put to ashes the Truth that ALL THAT GOD IS, HE IS.

It is impossible to be both God and man. This is duality and double-mindedness. It is totally unprofitable. Often one will say "I am God," and admit to having to grow into Truth, having to become "more spiritual" and so forth. This is a most subtle form of being double-minded. It is putting to ashes the Truth that GOD IS ALL. That YOU, who are reading this book, ARE GOD does not mean that you can lift up the status of your human identity to God status. You *cannot* take a limited, impoverished, mortal identity and proclaim it to be God. This indeed will cause confusion. The mortal identity with its entire history of accomplishments and failures must be seen for the nothingness it is and always has been. Seeing this clearly, you are left with nothing but witnessing your Self to be the very Presence of God.

Christ Jesus never adulterated His perfect nature by acknowledging that He was anything but the Presence of God: *"Have I been so long time with you, and yet hast thou not known me, Philip? he that hath seen me hath seen the Father..."* (John 14:9).

Jesus identified Himself *as* the Father – unlike metaphysicians (sincere though they be), who identify themselves as "one *with* the Father." The word "with" coordinates two separate entities, objects or identities. No matter how close together it draws these entities or identities, there are always two *somethings* there. One can be with a millionaire and not be a millionaire. And though they walk side by side, perhaps even arm in arm, the millionaire is still separate from his companion. God being Life, God being Love, God being Wisdom and God being Wealth is of no good to one who does not identify himself *as* God. Anything short of Divine Identification is sacrilegious. Anything short – even a hairsbreadth – of total Divine Identification is *false identification.* Only in the fiction of imagination can your Identity be put asunder. Moreover, everything else that is part and parcel of this mythical self is equally fiction – the illnesses, the feelings of futility, the failures, the discords, the loneliness, the despair, the lacks and limitations. They are all part of the biography of an identity that never had real being at all.

You, my friend, are joined with God (watch that four letter word) to such degree that you and God are indistinguishable – not that you're alike in any way, but you are the *same* Identity. One may look at you and call you Betty or Robert, but the label does not change the merchandise. You, Betty, are God. You, Robert, are God. You, reader, are God, and a name cannot obscure who and what you are. GOD IS ALL.

## "It Is Written, That Man Shall Not Live By Bread Alone, But By Every Word... Of God"

These were the words of Christ during His "temptations" in the wilderness, recorded in Matthew 4:4. When asked to turn stones into bread, He immediately replied, *"It is written, Man shall not live by bread alone, but by every word that proceedeth out of the mouth of God."* Herein is the lesson that is anathema to the mind-workers of popular metaphysics: Truth (God) cannot be used as a tool to demonstrate personal "of myself" power. Many of us have stepped over the thresholds of New Thought churches buoyed by the hope of finding a "tool" whose proper use would result in happiness, healing, money, companionship or even peace of mind. Mental, religious and philosophical keys are much like metal keys – they are easily lost. This system of teaching and thinking that focuses on tangible demonstrations of good is called "spiritual metaphysics," but it can more suitably be called the "Santa Claus God Syndrome." Those who seem to fall under this mesmerism would like to enjoy the fruits (bread) of spiritual revelation (The Word) without having experienced revelation (The Word).

In the Scriptures, "bread" signifies any and all forms of supply – not only that which we eat, but that which we wear and in which we live. Many devout worshippers of God (that have yet to identify themselves *as* God) have thought it necessary to take a vow of poverty and restriction to more fully demonstrate their spirituality. They have interpreted the quoted verse as, "Man shall not live by tangible good *at all*, but by every word that proceedeth out of the mouth of God." One cannot live the Life that is Spirit without living as evidence of ALL that God is. God is not in want of anything. God is not incomplete nor devoid of His substance; therefore man beholding his Self must evidence complete, needless living. It is much easier to see that this verse is really saying, "Man shall not live by every word that proceedeth out of the mouth of God, alone." The word "alone" needs stressing here. The "Word" is Revelation. Man cannot live by Revelation alone – devoid of *evidence* of that Revelation. Let us understand this word "Revelation." It is Truth Itself. It reveals *that which always has been*. Revelation changes nothing at all, and yet with Revelation (Truth) there is no desire for anything to be changed – at all. Some would say that manifestation *follows* Revelation. This *is not* Truth. Revelation, which is Truth Itself, *is* Manifestation. Furthermore, Revelation reveals the Eternal Manifestation.

To live by Revelation is to live as Truth Itself. Therefore let it suffice to say that nothing, *absolutely nothing* can be done, achieved or accomplished by mental or physical mechanics. All must be accomplished through the "hearing of the Word." Health must be achieved by Revelation of oneself as everpresent wholeness. Love must be achieved through Revelation that love is omnipresent existence. Peace must be achieved through Revelation of omnipresence. Financial security must be (and can be) achieved through Revelation of "All that the Father has I am, for the Father and I are one."

Revelation exposes the seemingly *missing* as already and eternally present. Nothing is really achieved or accomplished at all, but all is *revealed*.

Often there are reports of wonderful revelation and yet the evidence seems to be hidden or missing. This seems to occur as long as man thinks something is revealed to him and not AS him. If one maintains that Truth is revealed "to" him, he is separated from his revelation. One must be willing to KNOW that he IS presently and eternally every Truth revealed, because the Truth revealed discloses his real being.

None of this is contrary to that which is found in careful reading of the Scriptures. Jesus proclaims in John 6:48-51, *"I am that bread of life.... I am the living bread which came down from heaven...."* Again, *bread* is any and all tangible good – be it money, home, car, food, clothing, book, body or furniture. What is Jesus saying here? How does it relate to "living by bread?" These are simple questions and the answers are equally simple. One must experience the Revelation (Word) that he is (now) the very substance of every conceivable good imaginable *that he seems to be missing* in his mistaken sense of identity. When man correctly identifies himself as the Father, he will find that all that the Father has *he is*.

One could say that Revelation is "bread," in that it satisfies the needs of every man by revealing to him his needless state. And yet, Revelation does not come "to" man. Revelation (Truth Itself) is the *reality* of man. What seems to come "to" him is really seen to be his own eternal Identity. Moreover, Revelation shows itself as *visible evidence* of itself. But let's not be fooled here. Revelation does not produce satisfactory conditions; rather, it reveals that satisfactory conditions *have always been visibly and tangibly present*. Metaphysicians of the mental variety have as their sole aim the changing and improving of conditions. Where God is seen and known to BE ALL, there is nothing to change – only something to *perceive*.

*"As he* (Christ Jesus) *is, so are we in this world."* There is not a single one who cannot, right at this moment, proclaim himself to BE the bread of life. To actually perceive such Truth is to know that you are SELF-SUSTAINING, SELF-MAINTAINING and SELF-GOVERNING. It is clearly seen that there no longer need be a wait for someone (else) to grudgingly and reluctantly mete out to you such crusts of bread they may have. Perhaps it is employment you seem to need. Perhaps it is money. Maybe companionship and love seem to be absent. It could be that career advancement and job promotion seem thwarted by opposing personalities. It is here, via revelation of who and what you FACTUALLY are, that you are able to proclaim total freedom from dependency on people and things for that which seems to be missing – but which actually constitutes your very Identity. You, as the "bread of life," *are not* and *cannot* be separate and apart from your supply of all good. YOU ARE IT.

## "But, Whom Do You Say That I Am?"

After coming into Caesarea Philippi, Jesus in questioning His disciples asked: "Whom do people say that the Son of Man is?" Certainly rumors and speculations were being circulated abroad. After the disciples sputtered a few names, Jesus asked further: "But whom do you say that I am?"

Never, *ever* did Jesus announce a pure Truth of His identity speaking as individual man. Always it was as the voice of Universal

Omnipresence – Universal Omnipresence eternally unfazed by the assumptions and beliefs of mythical beings (human beings). The nature of Christ (Omnipresence Individualized) was not altered in any way by the talk of man "with breath in his nostrils." It was obvious that most of His disciples who had left home, friends and family to "follow" Him really did not perceive what manner of being He, Christ Jesus, was.

Right now, take a broader look at Jesus' question, "Whom do you say that I am?" Put Jesus the man far out of your mind now, and understand the "I am" to be the I AM THAT I AM (God). Do you imagine God (I AM) to be a gigantic personality – a *Who*? What is the nature of I AM? By Revelation, the answer to this comes forth: *"Flesh and blood did not* (could not) *reveal this to you, but my Father who is in heaven* (within you)..." (Matthew 16:17). Without Revelation we speculate as to the nature of I AM; however, I AM is not changed at all by our foolish speculation.

Ask yourself right now what it is that you believe God to be. Now drop all of these notions and begin again by asking your Self (the True and Only Omniscient Self) the same question. Are you willing right now to wait, if necessary, for Revelation of God's nature? Would you be more willing to invest your Self in your Self to know your Self's nature if you were aware that all seeming suffering was the false perception of God in action – the false perception of your Self? How much more willing *then* would you be to make this investment? Notwithstanding, this false perception of God in action is really *no activity at all*, since it is not God in action. Certainly it does *seem* real, but Revelation reveals what IS and EVERMORE SHALL BE.

Be more specific now. Whom do you say that you are? How are you identifying your Self? Do you say that your Self is male or female? Do you say that your Self is American, African or perhaps Portuguese? Are you, in your estimation, unemployed or employed? Are you possibly identifying your Self according to some line of activity – "I am a lawyer," "I am a doctor," "I am a secretary" and so on? Have you ever come forth boldly with wisdom declaring, "I am Christ?" What or who did hinder you? Was your stopping point due to judging from appearances? Flesh and blood (appearances) will not reveal your Self to you. God, your very own Being, knowing WHAT IT IS knows WHAT YOU ARE. God is in continual reverie rejoicing in the knowledge of His Identity. Ceasing from judging Self by appearances and asking your Self (God) what manner of being you ARE results in Divine Revelation, Divine Wisdom and Divine Knowledge of your True Identity. Do you believe this? Then you will seek for that Revelation in faith, knowing that it *must* be revealed to you because You already KNOW and already ARE the Truth revealed. This must be so, for GOD IS ALL.

Do you see that every description of yourself accessed by education and investigation serves only to limit the conscious awareness of your true Majesty, your true Glory, your true Beauty and your true Power? Every preconceived and inherited notion of your Self must be forsaken if the Self is to be consciously experienced. *"For this cause* (the experience of seeing and Being the One Presence) *shall a man leave father and mother* (all inherited concepts and notions of identity and human lineage)*, and shall cleave unto his wife* (awareness of pure Being)*: and the twain* (knowledge and manifestation) *shall be one flesh* (inseparable)*"* (Matthew 19:5). Now is the time when you must stand apart from the concepts of human beingness, of separate identities, of human birth and human living, of matter and material laws. As GOD IS ALL, and IS SPIRIT, none of these can be true.

The need for discovering the nature of God by Revelation cannot be overstated. God knowledge is Self knowledge. GOD IS ALL.

Philip greatly desired to see and know the Father. He had left all to follow Jesus and hoped that He could at least show him the Father. *"Lord, shew us the Father and it sufficeth us."* Note Jesus' response: *"Have I been so long time with you, and yet hast thou not known me, Philip? He that hath seen me hath seen the Father..."* (John 14:8-9). Jesus had spent much time with His disciples revealing to them what manner of Being they were: *"Ye are the light of the world."* They were not "of this world" of matter, of material laws, of humanity. *"Behold, the kingdom of God* (the Father) *is within you."* But Philip went on seeking the Father of the Jews – a Being far removed from His not-so-beloved creation. This was not the God of Christ Jesus, the God who not only was within Him but WAS HIM – AND IS HIM.

Humanity cannot behold the Christ. It takes an "other worldly" Being to behold the Christ. Do you seem to have great difficulty knowing your Self beyond your present sense of limitation – beyond limited power, limited ability, limited finances, limited happiness, limited peace, limited life? It is impossible to have the Revelation of your full Glory if you begin from the standpoint of humanhood. The human "i" cannot be lifted up from its grave of nothingness.

Whom and what do you say the Christ is? Is the Christ to you some ancient figure to be admired and adored? Is the Christ your higher self that you must grow into at some never *ever* time in the future? Or is Christ *now* your Everpresent Identity, such that you can *now* stand up and declare with absolute conviction, "He that seeth me seeth the Father"? GOD IS ALL.

## "This Kind Goeth Not Out But By Prayer And Fasting"

In Matthew 17:14-21 and Mark 9:14-2,9, we have a great story depicting the sense of powerlessness that sometimes seems to steal over us after we have reached tremendous demonstrable heights of spiritual awareness. At one point we rejoice confidently as did the seventy disciples: *"Even the devils* (most awesome appearances of evil) *are subject unto us through thy name."* Then at another point we question: *"Why could not we cast him* (false appearance) *out?"*

What power did Jesus possess that caused the spirits to depart? Was it a power not possessed by the disciples?

Knowledge was the power that put the dumb spirit to flight. Full and complete knowledge that God is really and truly ALL is indeed Power itself. It will put every contrary spirit to flight in the twinkling of an eye. "Where," you may ask, "did the dumb spirit go? Where do my problems, my concerns, my diseases, my lacks, my limitations, my restrictions, my confusions, my discords, my inharmonies, my poverty and my ignorance go upon the full and complete knowledge that GOD IS ALL?" It would be nothing less than poetic license to say that they "take wings and fly to the isle of nothingness from whence they came." But this leads one to believe that at some point they had reality, that at some point they had power. To answer truly and forthrightly, "They go nowhere." In the knowledge, in the *full* knowledge that GOD IS ALL, they are not seen, cognized or perceived to be *anything* or *any place* at all.

In 2 Kings 6:8-17, the story is told, and it is a wonderful story for illustrative purposes, that *"The king of Syria was warring with Israel."* Elisha the prophet had forewarned the king of Israel concerning the Syrian king's plan to attack, thus thwarting the aggressor's strategy. When the king of Syria learned that it was the prophet Elisha who had warned the Israelite king, he made specific plans to subdue Elisha.

*"Now when the attendant of the man of God* (Elisha) *had risen early and gone out, behold an army with horses and chariots was circling the city. The servant cried out to Elisha, 'Alas, my master! What shall we do?'"* Pay careful attention to Elisha's simple prayer: *"O, Lord, I pray, open his eyes that he may see."* The story concludes with, *"And the Lord opened the servant's eyes, and he saw; and behold, the mountain was full of horses and chariots of fire round about Elisha."*

Again, take particular note of Elisha's prayer. He did not ask for help or for deliverance from the appearance of evil. He did not ask for a route of escape. He never directed the prayer toward the appearance of offenders at all. He knew. Elisha knew something of the omnipotence of God as the *sole* Power and Presence. The appearance and suggestion of an opposing power did not daunt him in the least. He did, however, want his attendant to perceive what he himself perceived. Having eyes, the attendant did not see GOD AS ALL. Yet in the twinkling of an eye, his vision was "opened" to perceive the total impotency of the threat of evil. Evil is not a power. God is power. Moreover, God is the only power and *the only power possible*. This *must* be so for GOD IS ALL.

Jesus knew with unwavering certainty that God is all power. So when Pilate voiced his falsely assumed power either to crucify or release Him, Jesus was neither troubled nor afraid. Regarding Pilate, He knew that: *"Thou couldest have no power at all against me, except it were given thee from above...."* Furthermore, Jesus knew that He, but *not of himself*, was ALL POWER. Did He not identify Himself to Philip as the Father? This being Truth, Christ Jesus could boldly announce to the eleven disciples: *"All power is given unto me in heaven and in earth."*

Friend, reader, beloved! All Power is given unto you this day and forever in heaven (cause) and earth (manifestation). You are all power. Cease from identifying yourself as contained inside the glorious shell of your body. That is not all of you. To sense your entire identity is to sense that you are the *entirety* of Power; but again and again it must be said that this is not and cannot be Power *over anyone or anything*. This Power is the unhinderable ability to act in accordance with your nature. This is the unlimited ability to BE LOVE, to BE JOY, to BE PEACE and to BE YOURSELF.

All of the foregoing is true and is Truth; yet, at times it seems that there is the appearance of a condition that asserts itself with great intensity despite your best efforts to remain constant to all that God IS and you ARE. This is where the disciples were when they found that a particular "dumb spirit" was not subject unto their knowing.

Jesus explained to the perplexed disciples that certain appearances will seem to insist upon having some power in and of themselves, but they too must be seen for what they are: *"This kind goeth not out but by prayer and fasting"* (Matthew 17:21). To experience the Kingdom of heaven, which is the Kingdom of fulfillment, real and true prayer and fasting must be consistently and constantly practiced. Paul called it "praying without ceasing." This is a *must*, for certain appearances will not disappear unless one is *constantly* and *fully* aware that GOD IS ALL and ONLY GOD IS. Do not think that I am putting forth a system to reach or "tap into" a distant, who-knows-where God. Rather, I am urging a full recognition that ONLY GOD IS and ONLY WHAT GOD IS, IS EVIDENT. Abiding in and as this Truth, every false spirit of disease, distress, disaster and doom must vanish.

The eye that is single to the Truth that GOD IS ALL is the eye that lights the world. This is the vision that sees what IS and does not stop to ponder the appearances of what *isn't*.

Of all the so-called "spiritual practices," fasting is probably the most misunderstood and mispracticed. In many religious circles it is taught that one can obtain readily forthcoming answer to prayer if strict abstinence from food is observed while praying. Does it work? Perhaps if one believes strongly enough that it will, his belief will bring him a degree of satisfaction, and therefore it will seem to "work."

Why would man think that his human, material performances would or could ever affect God in any way? Would God be more God if one ate less? Do you see the absurdity of such a notion? According to this idea there would be no God at all, judging from the eating patterns of Americans alone. Also according to this false notion, starving nations would evidence the greatest manifestation of God's presence (and thus *would not manifest as starving nations)*. No form of human sacrifice is God-ordained; therefore, any kind of human sacrifice is totally ungodly.

*"To what purpose is the multitude of your sacrifices unto me? saith the Lord: I am full of the burnt offerings of rams and the fat of fed beasts; and I delight not in the blood of bullocks, or of lambs, or of he goats. When ye come to appear before me, who hath required this at your hand to tread my courts? Bring no more vain oblations; incense is an abomination unto me; the new moons and sabbaths... I cannot away with; it is iniquity.... Your new moons and appointed feasts my soul hateth; they are a trouble unto me; I am weary to bear them"* (Isaiah 1:11-14).

Further on, the prophet Isaiah espouses the true fast:

*"Is not this the fast I have chosen? to loose the bands of wickedness, to undo the heavy burdens and to let the oppressed go free and that ye break every yoke?"* (Isaiah 58:6).

Having done this:

*"Then shall thy light break forth as the morning and thine health shall spring forth speedily: and thy righteousness shall go before thee; the glory of the Lord shall be thy reward"* (Isaiah 58:8).

And:

*"The Lord shall guide thee continually, and satisfy thy soul in drought and make fat thy bones; and thou shalt be like a watered garden, and like a spring of water whose waters fail not.... And I will cause thee to ride upon the high places of the earth..."* (Isaiah 58:11-14).

The true fast is to abstain from every belief and idea of bondage, burden, oppression and evil. True fasting is the understanding of freedom as the everpresent, inexorable Fact of Existence.

The true fast is abstinence from every belief and idea of human, material, body and "natural" laws. All of these are varying names for the phantasmic law of restriction or limitation. The human law, which is no law at all, is the law of limited life, restricted ability, encroaching impotence and forced obsolescence. The material law, another non-law, reports that everything has a definite starting point and a definite stopping point (which translates to limitation). It tells often of what *can't* be done. It speaks of restricted performance and ability. Everything under this law also moves steadily toward its own demise. The law of the body is the law of death or non-existence. Under the law of the body, everything possible is done to prevent its sure, certain and eventual end – minus the belief that *this can indeed be accomplished*. Finally, that which is called "natural" law – nature's activity – brings only news of destruction. All of these supposed laws move toward nothingness – nothingness of life, nothingness of substance, and nothingness of body. Why? Because they, of themselves, are *nothing*. There is only one law – GOD IS ALL. This is not a law of restriction but the Law of Existence.

Are you willing to say and mean GOD IS ALL? This is fasting. Are you willing to say that because GOD IS ALL and God is Spirit, there are no human beings – that humanity even in its best form, does not and could not exist? This is fasting. Are you willing to claim no personal identity, life, mind, power or ability that God may be ALL LIFE, ALL MIND, ALL POWER, ALL ABILITY and ALL IDENTITY? This is fasting. Are you willing to see and say that there is no evil? This too is fasting. Are you willing to say death has no power, the grave has no power, time has no power and that no thing has power at all over or against the boundless, infinite YOU? This is the ultimate fast. Here, there is no mental grip on the idea of oppression at all. Oppression, restriction and limitation are free to go.

Certainly there are some conditions posing as reality itself that require something more than we have heretofore given. Where GOD IS ALL is eighty percent true with us, there remains twenty percent of untruth to seem real to us. That twenty percent phantom factor can appear in many guises. Perhaps it is depression and sadness one day. The next day it may seem to be disease and death. On another day it may seem to show as decay and destruction, violence and discord, loneliness and friendlessness. Perhaps like the disciples you are pondering, "Why won't these too be subject unto my knowing of Truth? What is it that I must do that I am not doing?" The answer, beloved, is total elimination of the phantom factor. GOD IS ALL must be one hundred percent. The answer to every seeming problem is GOD IS ALL. REALLY ALL. Full revelation of this Truth is the elimination of the phantom factor. This phantom factor is simply a seeming vacuum in the perception that GOD IS ALL. However, do not make the mistake of thinking that it has to be eliminated. It – the phantom factor – is nothing in and of itself, just as its offspring (every form of lack, limitation, restriction and death) is nothing. Deal only with the Omnipresent Something: GOD AS ALL. Everything must yield its supposed power to this Truth, for everything is seen to be no thing in the full Light of GOD IS ALL.

# Order Form

To order additional copies of *God is All*, please complete the
following form (all prices in US dollars):

Name: _____

Address: _____

City: _____ Prov./State: _____

Postal/Zip Code:_____ Telephone: _____


_____ copies @ $12.95:                              $_____

Shipping ($3.00 first book - $1.00 each add. book):   $_____

**Total amount enclosed:**                            **$_____**


Make cheques payable to *The Church of the Universal Christ*

Send to:    *The Church of the Universal Christ.*
            P.O. Box 39214
            Washington, D.C. 20016
            USA
            (202) 452-5589

PRIMERIO CARD CENTER

443-778300

John